AN UNFAIR ADVANTAGE

BUSINESS FUNDING SYSTEM

How to Crack the Code and
Beat the Banks at Their Own Game!

Get Any Business, Including Start-Ups, Approved
for "High Six-Figure" Unsecured Funding Fast,
Using Little-Known Underwriting Secrets
and Laser-Focused Stealth
Business Funding Techniques
You Will Never Learn from Anyone Else—

Not at Any Price!

John Garry

For permission requests, write to:
Permissions Coordinator
Eagle House Publications Inc.
1 Marina Circle North
Bella Vista, Arkansas 72715
+1 (888) 383-5318

Group Sales:

Special discounts are available on bulk purchases by corporations, associations, and organizations. Contact the publisher for details.

Printed in the United States of America

This publication is intended to share accurate and practical funding information. However, the author assumes no liability for losses, errors, or outcomes resulting from the use of this material. Readers should understand that results may vary. This book does not offer legal advice; readers should consult a qualified attorney for legal guidance.

Eagle House Publications, Inc.

ISBN 979-8-9998949-0-8

Dedication

To Jeannie:
My wife, my inspiration, my daily motivation,
and the love of my life.

Acknowledgments

Mr. Bill James, President of Wilshire Financial Group Inc., a loyal, dependable, and trusted good friend who has been by my side almost from the very beginning of the Wilshire project.

Mr. Cesar Osorio, Senior Managing Partner, the Rock, Mr. Dependable, an honest and good man, and our Ambassador of the Beverly Hills operations.

Ms. Yumna Sattar, my ever-patient and brilliant editor, flow and formatting contributor, and cover designer.

Ms. Carma Graber, my very talented copy and line editor and professional formatting and uploading expert.

To the entire **WFG financial team** in Beverly Hills and all our licensed satellite office leaders across the country, thank you for your relentless dedication.

Finally, my deep appreciation to **Mr. Henry Paderez** for 18 years of loyal and valued service. You will be missed.

My best wishes go with you, sir.

Contents

Dedication iii

Acknowledgments iv

Why This Is the Only Proven Business Funding System of Its Kind, and How It Will Transform Your Business and Your Life x

Chapter 1 xi

An Unfair Advantage: What the Banks Don't Want You to Know 1

    Inside the Machine: Cracking the Bank's New Code 4

    The Risk of Being Turned Down from a System You Don't Understand ... 7

Chapter 2 11

Choosing the Right Business Structure for Maximum Funding 11

    Why Corporate Credit Changes the Game, for Good 11

    Corporate Credit Is a Power Tool, Use It Like One 12

    Three Ways Corporate Credit Helps *Your* Personal Score 14

    Your Business Credit Isn't Just a Tool, It's Your Leverage 15

Chapter 3 19

Build It or Buy It, Your Business Foundation Starts Here 19

    Choosing the Right Business Structure 20

    Why Entrepreneurs Choose to Incorporate 20

    Starting from the Ground Up: What It Really Involves 21

    Cost Reality Check 21

    When to Start Fresh vs. When to Buy a Seasoned Company 21

    The Best States for Building Corporate Credit 22

    State-by-State Filing Fees and Annual Requirements: What You Will Pay and Where 23

    Final Reminder 27

    Filing with Confidence: Where to Register and Why It Matters 27

    A Word to the Wise on Filing Fees 33

    Naming Your Business: Strategic Language Wins Loans 34

    Registering Your Business 35

Obtaining an Employer Identification Number (EIN) 36

Two Critical Timelines You Must Nail... 36

Licenses and Permits: Strategy Matters 38

Opening Your Business Bank Account.. 38

The Importance of Your Initial Bank Deposit 39

Business Insurance: Don't Skip It 40

Business Plan: Do You Really Need It? 40

Do You Need Employees to Build Business Credit? 41

Keep Accurate Books from Day One 41

Marketing: Your Business Won't Sell Itself 42

Building a Strong Corporate Credit Foundation 42

Steps to Establish and Maintain Strong Business Credit 43

The Fast-Track: Purchasing a Seasoned Corporation........................... 45

Seamless Mergers with No Red Flags 46

Disadvantages of Forming a C Corporation 47

Recap: Why Corporate Credit Matters... 49

The Difference Between a D/B/A., a Limited Liability Company, and a
    Corporation.. 51

What Is a D/B/A?.. 51

What Is a Limited Liability Company (LLC)? 51

What Is a Corporation? 52

Final Considerations.. 53

Chapter 4 .... **55**

Obtaining Necessary Business Licenses and Permits **55**

The Business License 55

Zoning Permit... 56

Sales Tax Permit 56

Health Permit.. 56

Building Permit.. 57

Sign Permit 57

Professional License 57

Chapter 5 .... **59**

Business-Friendly Banks and the Not-So-Friendly **59**

The Importance of Opening a Separate Business Bank Account 59

Top Business-Friendly Banks for New Accounts 60

Choose Carefully 63

The S**t List: The Not-So-Friendly Bank 63

Chapter 6 65

Vendor Credit 65

Establishing Trade Credit with Vendors 65

Benefits of Vendor Credit Accounts 65

Ten Vendor Accounts That Offer Net- 30 Terms, ... 66

No Personal Guarantee Required 66

Chapter 7 69

Applying for Secured Business Credit 69

Applying for Secured Business Credit 69

Use Your Cards Responsibly! 72

Critical Warning 73

Chapter 8 74

The 10 Costliest Mistakes Entrepreneurs Make When Applying for

Business Funding 74

Stage 1: Unconscious Incompetence 76

Stage 2: Conscious Incompetence 76

Stage 3: Conscious Competence 76

Stage 4: Unconscious Competence 77

Mistake #1: Not Being Incorporated 78

Mistake #2: Having a Corporation That's Too New 79

Mistake #3: Your Corporation Is Suspended or Not in Good Standing .. 79

Mistake #4: Not Registering Your Corporation to Do Business in Your

State 80

Mistake #5: No Brick-and-Mortar Business Address 81

Mistake #6: No Business Telephone Number (and No 411 Listing) 82

Mistake #7: No Business Website (or a Website That You Built

Last Night) 84

Mistake #8: No Business Experian® Score or No Dun & Bradstreet®

Listing 86

Mistake #9: Not Having a Credit-Qualified Officer Sitting on Your Board of Directors 87

Mistake #10: Moving Forward Without Answers—The Silent Killer of Business Funding 90

Chapter 9 .... **94**

Building Credit with the Business Credit Reporting Bureaus **94**

How the PayDex® Score Works and Why It Matters 97

Building and Maintaining a Strong Business Credit Profile 100

Business Experian®, What They Track, and How It Affects You 104

Experian Business Credit Reporting® 104

Chapter 10 .... **109**

Managing Your Business Credit Profile **109**

Protecting Your Business Credit: Fraud, Errors, and Staying Ahead of Trouble 112

Monitoring Your Credit Reports the Right Way (Without Creating Problems) 116

The Truth About Trade Lines and Authorized Users, and Why Shortcuts Can Sometimes Backfire 120

Chapter 11 .... **125**

Applying for Corporate Credit Cards and Loans **125**

Preparing Your Business for Approval: Documents, Accuracy, and the Art of the Application 129

Choosing the Right Business Credit Cards: Strategy, Discipline, and Avoiding Costly Mistakes 133

Building Toward Bigger Approvals: Loans, Limits, and the Discipline That Gets You Funded 137

Mistake #1: Applying for the wrong products. 139

Mistake #2: Asking for too much too soon. 139

Mistake #3: Poor explanations for the use of funds. 140

Chapter 12 .... **143**

Expanding Your Business Credit Profile **143**

Expanding Business Through Corporate Lines of Credit Without Losing
Control 146

Using Equipment and Vehicle Leasing to Expand Without Straining Cash
or Credit 150

Strengthening Your Credit Through Banking Relationships and Payment
Discipline 153

Chapter 13 .... **159**

**Personal Guarantees: How They Can Affect Your Business and Your
Credit** **159**

How to Mitigate Risk When You Decide to Guarantee Business Debt
Personally 162

Co-Signing for Others: When It Makes Sense and When It Absolutely
Does Not 165

Why Personal Guarantees Became Standard and How to Protect
Yourself Going Forward 169

Chapter 14 .... **173**

**What's Happening Now, and How It Will Affect Your Business, Your
Credit, and Your Life** **173**

How This Moment Shapes Your Business, Your Credit, and Your Life 178

Chapter 15 .... **181**

Conclusion **181**

Independence Is Not a Theory, It's a Decision 183

Take Inventory: What Do You Know Now That You Didn't Know Before?
....186

The Choice That Remains Is Now Yours 188

Why This Is the Only Proven Business Funding System of Its Kind, and How It Will Transform Your Business and Your Life

"The woods are lovely, dark and deep, but I have promises to keep, and miles to go before I sleep."

—Robert Frost

Dear Entrepreneur,

The world is waiting for you, and I want you to get your business funded.

Whether you're starting a business, buying equipment, or scaling operations, this book will show you how to get the money you need.

It doesn't matter if your personal credit is excellent, fair, or struggling. Whether your business is 10 years old or 10 days, it doesn't matter. If you're tired of wasting time and getting rejected by banks, this book was written for you.

You now hold the keys to unlock the bank vault.

Inside this book, you will find funding guidelines, requirements, and strategies lenders don't discuss—the real methods that work behind the scenes. This isn't theory or advice from finance "gurus" who've never run a business. I've used these strategies to launch and fund multiple ventures over the past 50 years, generating millions of dollars annually.

The *Unfair Advantage Business Funding System* is battle-tested. It moves fast. It cuts through the BS and time-wasting nonsense. Everything I'm about to share has worked not just for me but also for thousands of our clients, helping them to secure millions in real business funding.

And yes, these techniques are still working right now.

I value your time and mine. That's why there is no filler in this book. No unrealistic promises. Every strategy here is legal, tested, and field-proven. You will discover how to outmaneuver traditional lenders with smart preparation and strategic moves that most business owners never learn. Bankers know these guidelines and funding tactics, but will never tell you.

This is exactly why the national business loan approval rate hovers around just 39 percent.

I wrote this book to change that, for you.

Whether you need funding to launch your dream or expand your team, you will learn how to apply for business credit and get approved. Fast.

This is your roadmap to the money.

I hope you enjoy reading it as much as I've enjoyed writing it. To your success, I remain sincerely yours,

John R. Garry

Chapter 1

An Unfair Advantage: What the Banks Don't Want You to Know

"Pay no attention to that little man behind the curtain. I am the Mighty Wizard of Oz!"

—The Wizard of Oz

Let's get one thing straight: some bankers don't like what we do. And you know what? That doesn't hurt my feelings. In fact, I'm perfectly fine with that.

I remember the call vividly. I was in our Beverly Hills office, Wilshire Financial Group headquarters, when one of our prospective clients rang me up. She'd been speaking with a VP loan processor at a small bank in Madison, Wisconsin. Innocent conversation, until the name "Wilshire Financial Group" came up. Then the mood shifted. Fast.

That banker had plenty to say. According to the prospective client, the conversation went something like this:

"We don't like what John Garry and his team are doing. They're providing confidential underwriting info, creating corporations deliberately engineered to beat our systems. They're giving their clients "an unfair advantage over the bank."

Let me translate that for you: *The Banker was upset because we understood the bank's computer approval program probably better than he did.*

That VP didn't accuse us of fraud. He didn't say we lied or cheated. What rattled him was that we told the truth, loudly, and gave people access to the kind of high-level funding strategies banks don't want you to know exist. That wasn't unfair. That was reality. We pull the curtain back and show our clients exactly what is going on. And that's exactly what I'm about to do in this book.

This information is not being provided for the faint of heart or the thumb-sucking set. If you need a lot of coddling, you're reading the wrong book. But if you're ready to cut to the chase, get your funding applications approved quickly, without all the runaround, without excuses, and without delay, then welcome. You're in the right place.

We don't make promises we can't keep. The system we teach is 100 percent legal. It's sharp, efficient, and unconventional. You won't find this information being taught in business schools, and no traditional lender's going to sit down, hold your hand, and spell it out for you. Why would they? Their job is to follow the lending guidelines and protect the bank's money.

Now, about that *"unfair advantage"* the banker mentioned …

Let's be adults. Life isn't fair. Banks rewrote the rulebook after the 2007 financial meltdown. They ripped the human element out of the lending process and replaced it with a computer program. Computers don't care how passionate you are or how good your business plan looks. You don't get to charm your way into a loan anymore. You get the opportunity, just one time, to meet the bank's guidelines and benchmarks.

So we teach people how to meet them.

What rattled that banker wasn't that we gamed the system; it's that we learned it inside out. We know what works. We know what gets flagged. We know the timing, the sequencing, the details, the guidelines, and the bank's loan thresholds that get real businesses approved.

It's not cheating. It's competence. We will show you exactly how to navigate the maze, complete the loan applications correctly, and get your business funded fast.

We don't waste time. We don't rely on loopholes. What we do is show hardworking entrepreneurs how to present themselves properly in front of a computer program that only respects structure, readiness, and exact precision.

And that's the point the banker missed.

We're not anti-bank. In fact, we respect all our lenders who are smart, forward-thinking, and know how to quickly spot a good file and loan application. We just don't waste time playing by outdated rules and guidelines when we know that they have already been updated and changed.

If you've been turned down before, told *"you're not ready,"* or heard some vague excuse from a guy in a suit, sitting behind a big desk in the bank, buckle up. I'm about to walk you through the entire loan process, no nonsense, no BS, and no apologies.

Because no, Mr. VP from Wisconsin, it's not "unfair."

It's just businessmen who now know the current lending guidelines, are prepared to meet all of them, and are smarter and more informed than, apparently, you were expecting.

Inside the Machine: Cracking the Bank's New Code

Let's be clear: the game changed when the banks replaced people with algorithms. After the 2007 subprime meltdown, it stopped being about trust and handshake deals. The smiling loan officer behind the desk became irrelevant. Now it's all about what the software sees. It's binary. Clean. Cuts right to the chase, and predictable, *if you understand it.*

That's where my team and I come in. Our clients aren't getting loans because they know someone at the bank. They're getting loans because we teach them to speak the computer's language. We have carefully analyzed the bank's unsecured business loan approval computer program. Now we teach it to our clients. Step by step.

Banks don't hand out money based on potential. They don't care if you "really need it" or if your business plan has vision. They care about the loan being paid back, on time, with interest. Does your business meet the bank guidelines? Is your business structured properly, and is it seasoned? Does it have a trail of data that matches their internal compliance checklist? The only question that matters is: Does your file and business loan application meet all the requirements the algorithm is looking for?

We make sure that the answer is yes. We've built a system to match that criteria precisely. It's clean, it's legal, and it's built on real field-tested experience. Not hypotheticals and not theories. Over the last 19+ years, we've helped thousands of clients get their business funding approved for millions of dollars. We've seen the trends. We've adjusted. We've stayed 10 steps ahead. And the results speak for themselves.

Now let's address the common assumptions, the things people *think* will help their application and absolutely won't.

Trade lines? My advice is don't touch them.

Authorized user accounts? Stay away. I'll explain this in more detail in the following pages.

Faking documents to inflate credit strength? Don't even think about it.

You don't need gimmicks. You need a good, solid structure. A clean file. Real data that makes sense under scrutiny. That's what our system delivers.

The Wilshire Financial Group doesn't teach loopholes. We teach lender-approved business frameworks. Clients often come to us after wasting time and money on so-called "credit repair" gurus. They've spent thousands of dollars buying garbage: sketchy trade lines, template letters, or secret backdoor hacks. None of it works to get your horse across the finish line. It's nonsense, unnecessary, and collapses the second a real underwriter takes a closer look.

Banks can sniff that stuff out instantly. And once they flag your business, you're done. Not just for that loan, with that bank, but possibly with all other banks for six months or longer.

We don't play games.

Instead, we help clients build their business structure and loan applications from the ground up with one goal in mind: Meet or exceed every underwriting guideline from day one.

That's why we build *seasoned corporations*, fully legal, established business entities engineered to get you funded fast. These companies have age, documentation, clean compliance records, and the right industry codes. They're built to win and check all the boxes on the bank's internal computer checklist.

When a banker calls that *"an unfair advantage,"* what they really mean is: *"How do you know all this?"*

The bottom line here is …

We're not breaking any rules. We're operating within them, better than most bank loan officers even understand. We've worked for many years with the lending world. We've seen the back-end systems. We've been privy at times to memos that never go public. We've been in this business for decades. That knowledge doesn't belong on a shelf.

It belongs in the hands of hard-working, real business entrepreneurs who need positive funding results.

Let's break down what else we actually *do* for our clients, because there is a lot of misinformation out there.

We don't just hand someone a checklist and wish them luck. We walk them through every part of the process, every form, every compliance box, every underwriting angle. We dig into what kind of funding they need, what kind of repayment plan makes sense, and what their real funding timeline is. Then we engineer the profile to match the seasoned corporation, should they need one to meet the company age requirements.

That means we analyze their business structure. We review their existing paperwork. We clean up anything sloppy or inconsistent. We even advise them on how to build a credible repayment plan and how to present it should they be asked. By the time they apply for the business loan, their file doesn't just "look good," it *is* good, and it's bulletproof.

That's the difference between what we do and what some quick-buck online gurus promise.

And let's talk about our clients. They're not trying to scam the system. They're good, hard-working people. Smart, driven entrepreneurs who want to fund their dreams. They're often frustrated, stuck in a cycle of loan rejections, not because they're unqualified, but because no one's ever shown them how the banking loan application process really works.

We changed that.

Before we move forward with anyone, we vet them. We look at their experience, their goals, and, most importantly, their character. We're not in the business of gambling with our lenders' trust. We only bring clients we believe in to our banks. It's how we've maintained long-term relationships with the same lending partners for nearly two decades.

We value our lenders. They know us. They trust us. And in turn, they trust the people we bring them. That trust isn't bought, it's earned. One accurate file at a time.

Which brings us back to our banker friend from Wisconsin … He wasn't angry because we were bending the rules. He was angry because we were teaching people how to play by them, with precision. If that's what he calls an unfair advantage?

Then I'll call bulls**t … It's just being prepared and doing things right.

The Risk of Being Turned Down from a System You Don't Understand

Let's talk about what banks *don't* want to advertise: their biggest fear isn't fraud, it's loss.

Statistically, **65 percent of small businesses fail within the first five years**. You don't hear that number from lenders very often, but trust me, they know it. They *plan* around it. That's why most traditional lenders won't even look at a loan request from a business less than three years old. Doesn't matter how smart you are, how good your product is, or how convincing your pitch might be. If you're under three years old in business? The answer is no loan for you.

This is what I call **The 3–5 Year Factor**, and if you're not accounting for it in your funding strategy, you're just wasting your time.

So here is the reality check: Walk into a bank with a brand-new LLC and a beautiful pitch deck, ask for a startup loan, and what you're going to hear next is the financial equivalent of *"No soup for you!"*

That's not personal. That's reality. And that's why our model works.

The Wilshire Financial Group doesn't just prepare clients; we get them funded. If their business isn't old enough to meet traditional lending age requirements, we give them access to our inventory of *seasoned corporations*. These are real entities, built right, aged on the shelf, and verified to meet or exceed the internal guidelines lenders quietly rely on. They give your application the age, credibility, and risk profile it needs to pass the first level of automated rejection.

We've submitted thousands of clients into our business funding programs. Not one has ever been turned down for funding for any fault of the company. Not one client. That's not just luck. That's just planning in advance and good corporate engineering.

And before anyone throws around any accusations, let me be crystal clear: none of this is illegal. Not even close. There is no deception here, no hidden traps. Our clients don't lie, and we never suggest that they do. In fact, we *explicitly* reject anyone who thinks there is room for dishonesty in this process.

We don't allow our clients to make false claims. We don't tell people to hide liabilities. It's nonsense, it's not necessary, and it's potentially fraudulent.

What we offer is **knowledge**. We guide entrepreneurs on how to build a business profile that's not only fundable, but sustainable. We teach them the importance of being completely honest with potential lenders, prepared, and structured in a way that aligns with what lenders want to see. It's not about gaming the system. It's about finally understanding it.

You want to get your business funded? Great. First, you must learn the rules.

That's where my Wilshire Financial team enters the picture. I'm providing you now: the playbook. So is this an *"unfair advantage,"* as the banker from Wisconsin called it?

Think about it. If an entrepreneur hires a team of experts to help them understand and prepare a funding strategy that meets the bank's internal expectations … if that team walks them through every compliance step, guides them on how to establish a properly structured business entity, and helps them avoid the landmines that sink most applications … that's not unfair, that's just good business planning.

Banks have armies of lawyers and risk officers behind their application systems. You think they don't have their system down?

Let's not be naive.

The bank has too much to lose.

If giving someone access to my 50+ years of banking, funding, and underwriting experience, plus the knowledge my entire WFG team of financial business experts has accumulated from working directly *with* lenders for nearly two decades, is somehow considered "unfair," then maybe that banker should reconsider who he wants to serve.

We don't fear scrutiny. We welcome it. Our process holds up under review because it was built that way. And we'll keep doing what we do for as long as business owners are out there fighting for their financial future, only to have their business loan application rejected by a system they were never taught how to navigate. You want to know why I wrote this book?

Because I've had enough of watching smart, hardworking entrepreneurs get turned down for the funding they desperately need to make their business dreams come true, not because they lack vision, but because they lack *access*.

Access to knowledge. Access to professional guidance. Access to a computer-program funding system designed by banks and rarely, if ever, explained to business owners.

I'm not going to watch that happen anymore. So no, this isn't a book about loopholes. This isn't a cheat sheet. This is a roadmap to the money. The truth, stripped down, raw, and unapologetic. You want to build a business? You're going to need money. You want to get bank funding? You need to know the rules and the guidelines?

Keep reading, and let's get to work.

Chapter 2

Choosing the Right Business Structure for Maximum Funding

*"When people don't understand something, they say 'no' or
'you can't do that,' when all they really mean is: 'I don't know
how to do that.'"*

— **Alexanderism**

Why Corporate Credit Changes the Game, for Good

It doesn't matter what business you're in, or even what kind of business you want to be in. Are you serious about growth, funding, or ever wanting to scale? You're going to need a corporate business structure.

Here is the reality: You can either start one now and build corporate credit slowly over time (we're talking three years of patient and consistent effort), or you can purchase a seasoned corporation from a trusted source and start applying for funding immediately. Either path works. One just works *faster*.

But this isn't just about getting access to money. Corporate credit, when built properly, becomes your business's silent workhorse. It opens doors, builds credibility, and protects your personal financial life if you know how to use it correctly. Blow it off, treat it like a side task, or worse, misuse it, and you will set your business success back years and maybe, permanently.

Corporate Credit Is a Power Tool, Use It Like One

Here is the thing: Once your business has an established credit profile, you've got leverage. Lenders view you as a calculated risk they can understand. Suppliers start extending better terms. And investors pay attention. None of this happens when you're mixing your personal and business finances into one fragile, disorganized mess.

Corporate credit is *not* a clone of your personal credit score. It's a totally separate credit identity, one that stands on its own. It's your business's reputation in the financial world. And if you build it strong from the start, it can become one of your greatest assets.

Let's break down exactly what good credit brings to the table.

Access Capital When You Actually Need It

This is the big one. Once your corporate credit is in place, you will soon be able to stop depending on personal guarantees for every business decision. You become fundable *as a business.*

With a solid credit profile, banks, lenders, and private institutions are more willing to extend business lines of credit, working capital loans, equipment financing, and expansion funds. You will get more yeses and at much better terms. That means lower interest rates, longer repayment windows, and more capital available without groveling.

That kind of liquidity gives you agility: You can jump on new opportunities, cover short-term gaps, and scale when the time is right.

Improve Cash Flow Without Sacrificing Equity

Building corporate credit doesn't just get you access to funds; it also changes how you run your business.

Need to make a large inventory purchase? Extend your supplier terms instead of draining your cash. Need breathing room during a seasonal lull? Tap a credit line that keeps operations smooth. All of this helps you **preserve ownership** and avoid giving up equity just to stay afloat.

Even better, vendors and suppliers are more willing to negotiate favorable terms when they see your business has an established payment history. You're no longer treated like a risk; they'll fight to keep your business.

Protect Your Personal Credit and Personal Assets

Mixing your personal credit with business expenses is a recipe for long-term damage. One downturn in sales and your personal score tanks along with your business credit score. One late payment from a client or tenant, and suddenly your mortgage loan is on shaky ground.

A properly structured corporation with its own credit profile changes that. It creates **legal and financial separation** between you and your business. That means your personal credit isn't jeopardized every time your business makes a move. It also protects your personal assets in the event your business ever hits legal or financial turbulence.

Let the corporation take the heat, that's what it's built for.

Build a Reputation That Opens Doors

A business with an established credit record earns respect, plain and simple.

Suppliers trust you. Lenders see stability. Certification agencies take you seriously. Even potential partners and investors look at your credit profile as part of their due diligence. It becomes part of your reputation, proof that youre not just another idea guy with a dream, but a businessperson who knows how to play the game and is responsible.

Some industries even require financial certifications before granting certain licenses or contracts. A strong business credit profile is the first step to opening those doors that stay locked to hobbyists and side hustlers.

Three Ways Corporate Credit Helps *Your* Personal Score

Here is the part no one tells you: Building strong corporate credit can actually improve your *personal* credit too. Here is how:

1. **Reduced Personal Credit Usage:** When you stop putting business expenses on personal cards, your credit utilization drops. That alone can give your personal score a serious upward bump.

2. **Loan Approval Leverage:** If you apply for funding and your business credit looks great, even if your personal credit's just average, you will be seen as a lower risk. Strong business credit helps offset a weaker personal score.

3. **Enhanced Financial Credibility:** Lenders and credit bureaus take notice when your business is responsible with its

debt. That credibility reflects positively on you as the owner and can lead to lower personal interest rates and better offers.

Your Business Credit Isn't Just a Tool, It's Your Leverage

A solid business credit profile isn't just a way to get funding; it's your company's financial résumé. It determines what you qualify for, how much you will pay, and how far you can go. When it's strong, doors swing open. When it's weak, even basic necessities become uphill battles.

Let's talk specifics.

Accesses Capital When You Need It Most

With strong business credit, you can access everything from equipment loans and working capital lines to high-limit business credit cards. This gives you flexible funding to manage expenses, cover emergencies, or seize sudden opportunities without draining your operating cash.

Builds a History That Works in Your Favor

Using business credit cards or accounts responsibly and paying on time builds a favorable credit profile. That history isn't just a number; it's proof to lenders that you're trustworthy, and it unlocks access to larger loans and much better rates over time.

Gives You an Actual Credit Score, With Impact

Your business credit score, tracked by agencies like Dunn & Bradstreet and Experian Business, is what lenders, vendors, and even insurers use to evaluate your company's financial behavior. The better your credit score, the better your loan terms, rates, and, of course, your business loan approval odds.

Provides Emergency Buffer When the Unexpected Happens

Bad month? Sudden expense? Market shift? A line of credit can save your business from panic mode. Instead of scrambling, you lean on your established credit while you get things back under control.

Fuels Growth, Without Diluting Ownership

Need to expand, launch a new product, or open a second location? Strong business credit gives you access to financing that doesn't involve giving up equity in your company or taking on personal risk.

Offers Perks, Rewards, and Practical Value

Let's not ignore the extras. Business credit cards often offer real perks, cash back, line of credit checks, travel rewards, airline upgrades, free flights, discounts, and in some cases, yes, even a shiny toaster for your break room. We've gotten plenty of bank perks over the years. If you're spending anyway, why not make it work for you?

What Happens When Your Credit Is Weak, or Nonexistent?

Now here is the other side of the coin. Letting your credit go unmanaged or worse, misusing it, can bury your business and your personal finances in ways most people don't realize until it's too late.

Loan Approvals Become a Grind

Low scores mean either flat-out denials or high-interest approvals that feel more like punishments than partnerships. Forget favorable terms, you will be lucky to get any offer that doesn't bleed you dry.

Higher Interest = More Debt = Slower Growth

A weak credit score makes you more "risky" in the eyes of lenders. That means higher rates, stricter terms, and more money going to interest instead of operations. Compound that over time, and it becomes a slow financial bleed.

You Will Be Locked Out of Most Real Credit Opportunities

You might not even get approved for a business credit card, let alone a business loan. Need a car for your operations? Expect massive down payments or denials. Want to lease a small office space? Landlords will check your score. You may be out before you've even stepped in.

You Will Be Asked for Security Deposits, Everywhere

Utilities, phone service, internet providers, and even landlord leases may require hefty deposits just because your credit score isn't up to par. It's money wasted just to prove you're not a liability.

Your Insurance Premiums Will Spike

Fair or not, insurers often base business (and even personal) premiums on credit history. A poor score signals risk, and they charge you accordingly.

Employment May Even Be at Risk

In many industries, employers check credit reports as part of the hiring process. A bad score can reflect poorly on your judgment, responsibility, and reliability. Is it always fair? No. But it's a fact of life, and it's happening.

Renting Can Become a Dead End

Looking for a commercial lease or even a personal rental? Landlords run credit checks, and poor scores often mean rejections or demands for co-signers and extra fees. That new office space or storefront you had your eye on? It might be out of reach before you even get a foot in the door.

Starting or Scaling a Business Becomes Harder

If your credit is shot, your ability to fund your startup or grow an existing venture drops significantly. Investors get wary, banks say no, and even crowdfunding can suffer once people get a peek behind the curtain.

Car Loans and Credit Cards Become Cost Traps

Need a company vehicle? Expect ridiculous interest or impossible terms. Planning on applying for a new credit line? Prepare to be denied, or hit with sky-high rates and fees. The system doesn't forgive easily when you've let your business credit profile fall apart.

Bottom line: Your business and personal credit will either lift you or limit you. It's not about gaming the system; it's about *understanding* it and putting yourself in a position to win. So if you're reading this book and wondering where to begin: Start with building a strong, fundable business profile and credit rating. Every other strategy in this book hinges on that one decision. Let's move forward from here, with a solid foundation built and the credit blind spots gone.

Chapter 3

Build It or Buy It, Your Business Foundation Starts Here

"Socialism isn't going to stop the selfishness of human behavior. It isn't going to stop the greed. If you take 20 dollars and give a dollar to every sonuvabitch in a room and come back a year later, one of those bastards will have most of the money. It's just human nature, and you're not going to whip it with a lot of laws."

— John Wayne

So, let's get straight to it.

If you're reading this chapter with the clear goal of raising serious capital, anywhere from $250,000 to $1 million in the next few months, your best move isn't to start from scratch. You will want a **seasoned, aged corporation or LLC** that's in good standing and is at least three years old. That age benchmark is the unspoken minimum for serious funding approval. And yes, there are legal ways to acquire one, methods I'll outline later in this book.

However, if your timeline is flexible and you're not looking for major funding just yet, you have another path available: **Form your own company and build its credit profile over time**. It's less expensive upfront, but it requires one thing most people don't have: **patience**.

Let's walk through what it takes to go the DIY route and build corporate credit from the ground up.

Choosing the Right Business Structure

The first big decision? Legal structure. You've got options—sole proprietorship, partnership, LLC, or corporation—but for our purposes, and especially for business funding, you've only got two real contenders: the LLC or the corporation.

Here is why: Both offer liability protection, funding flexibility, and credibility with lenders. Sole proprietorships and partnerships may be less expensive and easier to start, but they won't get you far in the credit game and will leave you exposed to personal liability. If you're serious about building a fundable business, start with a structure that lenders respect.

Why Entrepreneurs Choose to Incorporate

Smart entrepreneurs don't just incorporate for the tax write-offs. They do it because it sends a message to lenders, clients, investors, and vendors that you mean business. Incorporating gives you:

- Better access to funding

- Limited personal liability

- A professional public image

- More favorable taxation treatment

So yes, there is paperwork. Yes, there are fees. But done right, it's an investment, not an expense.

Starting from the Ground Up: What It Really Involves

I'll outline and go over the steps you need to take to form your business, build its identity, and lay the credit groundwork properly. That includes a **state-by-state breakdown** of incorporation fees and annual maintenance requirements. Whether you're forming an LLC or a C-corp, you need to know what you're committing to, not just in money, but in time.

Cost Reality Check

Depending on where you file, incorporating might cost you as little as $50 … or as much as several hundred dollars up front. Some states throw in surprise fees and documentation requirements that complicate things further. And it doesn't stop there. You will likely have **annual report fees, franchise taxes, and compliance forms** to deal with every year. Those costs vary from $25 to over $500, depending on your state. Keep reading for specifics.

But let me be absolutely clear: **Your highest cost is time**. If you're starting from scratch and planning to raise serious money, you're looking at a **minimum three-year wait** before most lenders will consider your company fundable. That's three years of clean books, on-time payments, and flawless compliance.

Time is money. How much of it can you afford to spend?

When to Start Fresh vs. When to Buy a Seasoned Company

Look, there is no one-size-fits-all answer here. If you're running a local business, you aren't in a rush for funding, and you want to control everything from day one, building from the ground up makes sense. You will save money and get to know every corner of your business. But if your primary goal is to secure funding fast and make moves in the next three to six months, **buying an established corporation** may be a much better strategic move. That's what many of our clients do, especially those seeking rapid results with maximum impact. Still not sure? That's why I'm here. One-on-one consultations are available for readers who've purchased this guide and want my personal, tailored advice based on their funding goals and the nature of their business.

The Best States for Building Corporate Credit

Not all states are created equal when it comes to ease, cost, and flexibility of incorporation.

If you want the best shot at maximizing credit-building potential, getting larger loan approvals, *and* keeping your maintenance obligations low, I recommend sticking with one of these five states:

1. Delaware

2. Florida

3. Texas

4. Colorado

5. Arkansas

Each of these states has favorable laws for corporations and lender-receptive reputations. If you're serious about building maximum business credit and minimizing objections, this list should be your short list.

Of course, some readers may still choose to incorporate in their home state, and that's fine too, but be aware of the cost and compliance responsibilities that come with that decision. Also be aware that regardless of which state you decide to incorporate in, you will still need to foreign file your corporation or LLC in the state in which you reside and are going to be doing business.

State-by-State Filing Fees and Annual Requirements: What You Will Pay and Where

Whether you're filing in your home state or incorporating in one of the "big five" maximum funding states I recommended (Delaware, Florida, Texas, Colorado, or Arkansas), you need to know exactly what it's going to cost, both up front and year over year.

Here is your state-by-state breakdown of incorporation filing fees and annual maintenance fees. Use this section as your cheat sheet before making any moves. **Note:** These are baseline fees at the time of printing and may not reflect expedited processing charges or additional service fees. Requirements and costs can change, so double-check with your Secretary of State or call our Beverly Hills office for the latest updates.

State	Filing Fee	Annual Report Fee	Notes / Cautions
Alabama	$200	$100	
Alaska	$250	$100	
Arizona	$50	$45	
Arkansas	$50	$150	Highly regarded, fast-growing lending and credit-building benefits.

State			
California	$100	$25	Labor-intensive and fee-heavy, FTB demands frequent filings.
Colorado	$50	$10	
Connecticut	$250	$150	
Delaware	$89	$50	Highly recommended for credit building and investor credibility.
Florida	$125	$150	Top-tier credit-building state with streamlined reporting.
Georgia	$100	$50	
Hawaii	$50	$15	
Idaho	$100	$0	
Illinois	$150	$75	
Indiana	$95	$31.25	
Iowa	$50	$60	
Kansas	$165	$50	
Kentucky	$40	$15	
Louisiana	$75	$30	
Maine	$145	$85	

Maryland	$100	$300	High annual fees may outweigh credit-building benefits.
Massachusetts	$275	$125	
Michigan	$60	$25	
Minnesota	$155	$0	
Mississippi	$50	$0	
Missouri	$58	$25	
Montana	$70	$20	
Nebraska	$105	$10	
Nevada	$75 + $500 License Fee	$150 + $500 Annual Business Fee	Most expensive overall; consider only for strategic reasons.
New Hampshire	$100	$100	
New Jersey	$125	$50	
New Mexico	$100	$0	
New York	$125	$9	
North Carolina	$125	$200	
North Dakota	$135	$50	

Ohio	$99	$50	
Oklahoma	$100	$25	
Oregon	$100	Varies	
Pennsylvania	$125	$70	
Rhode Island	$230	$50	
South Carolina	$135	$0	
South Dakota	$150	$50	Recommended for ease of filing and low regulatory burden.
Tennessee	$100	$50	
Texas	$300	$0	Top recommendation: highly business-friendly.
Utah	$70	$15	
Vermont	$125		Annual report info not listed.
Virginia	$100	$50	
Washington	$180	$60	
West Virginia	$100	$25	

Wisconsin	$100	$25	
Wyoming	$100	$50	

Final Reminder

Fees change. Processes shift. Forms get updated. Before filing, make sure to verify details directly with the Secretary of State in your chosen jurisdiction, or contact **Eagle House Publications** at **1+ (888) 383-5318** to be connected with one of our Wilshire Financial Group advisors. We stay up-to-date on the latest requirements and funding criteria, the call is free, and we're here to help.

Filing with Confidence: Where to Register and Why It Matters

You've decided to form a corporation. You know which states give you the most funding leverage. Now comes the tactical move, filing. It sounds administrative and boring. But don't let the routine nature of this step fool you. **How and where you file will set the tone for every lender interaction that follows.** This part is about positioning. It's about getting yourself into the system with precision, not paperwork fatigue.

Across all 50 US states, and yes, US territories too, each Secretary of State has its own quirks: fees, filing portals, annual reporting windows, processing times. Some states roll out the red carpet. Others? They throw up hurdles. If you've got the time and stamina, you can file yourself. If not, work with us or a company that knows how to push this through without friction.

For convenience, this section includes **a fully updated directory** of every Secretary of State's office in the country, mailing addresses, phone numbers, and the works. Use it. Don't guess. Don't Google blindly and hope you land on the right form. Call. Confirm. Submit the right documents the first time.

State/Territory	Address	City, State ZIP	Phone
Alabama	PO Box 5616	Montgomery, AL 36103-5616	(334) 242-7200
Alaska	550 W 7th Ave, Ste 1535	Anchorage, AK 99501-3587	(907) 465-2500
Arizona	1700 W Washington St, Floor 7	Phoenix, AZ 85007	(602) 542-4285
Arkansas	Executive Office State Capitol, Ste 256, 500 Woodlane Ave	Little Rock, AR 72201	(501) 682-1010
California	1500 11th St	Sacramento, CA 95814	(916) 653-6814
Colorado	1700 Broadway, Ste 200	Denver, CO 80290	(303) 894-2200
Connecticut	30 Trinity St	Hartford, CT 06106	(860) 509-6200
Delaware	Division of Corporations, PO Box 898	Dover, DE 19903	(302) 739-3073

Florida	A. Gray Building, 500 S Bronough St	Tallahassee, FL 32399-0250	(850) 245-6500
Georgia	214 State Capitol	Atlanta, GA 30334	(844) 753-7825
Guam	Ricardo J. Bordallo Governor's Complex	Adelup, Guam 96910	(671) 472-8931
Hawaii	DCCA Business Registration Division, PO Box 40	Honolulu, HI 96810	(808) 586-2727
Idaho	450 N 4th St	Boise, ID 83702	(208) 334-2301
Illinois	213 State Capitol	Springfield, IL 62756	(800) 252-8980
Indiana	200 W Washington St, Room 201	Indianapolis, IN 46204	(317) 232-6531
Iowa	First Floor, Lucas Building, 321 E 12th St	Des Moines, IA 50319	(888) 767-8683
Kansas	Memorial Hall, 1st Floor, 120 SW 10th Ave	Topeka, KS 66612-1594	(785) 296-4564

Kentucky	700 Capital Ave, Ste 152	Frankfort, KY 40601	(502) 564-3490
Louisiana	PO Box 94125	Baton Rouge, LA 70804-9125	(225) 925-4704
Maine	148 State House Station	Augusta, ME 04333-0148	(207) 626-8400
Maryland	16 Francis St	Annapolis, MD 21401	(410) 974-5521
Massachu-setts	One Ashburton Pl, 17th Floor	Boston, MA 02108	(617) 727-9640
Michigan	Department of State	Lansing, MI 48918	(888) 767-6424
Minnesota	60 Empire Dr, Ste 100	St. Paul, MN 55103	(877) 551-6767
Mississippi	401 Mississippi St	Jackson, MS 39201	(601) 359-1350
Missouri	600 W Main St	Jefferson City, MO 65101	(573) 751-4936
Montana	Capitol Building, Room 260, PO Box 202801	Helena, MT 59620-2801	(406) 444-2034
Nebraska	PO Box 94608	Lincoln, NE 68509-4608	(402) 471-2554
Nevada	101 N Carson St, Ste 3	Carson City, NV 89701	(775) 684-5708

New Hampshire	Corporation Division, 107 N Main St	Concord, NH 03301-4989	(603) 271-3246
New Jersey	PO Box 300	Trenton, NJ 08625	(609) 777-2581
New Mexico	Capitol Annex North, 325 Don Gaspar, Ste 300	Santa Fe, NM 87501	(800) 477-3632
New York	123 William St	New York, NY 10038-3804	(518) 473-2492
North Carolina	PO Box 29622	Raleigh, NC 27626-0622	(919) 814-5400
North Dakota	600 E Boulevard Ave, Dept 108	Bismarck, ND 58505-0500	(701) 328-2900
Ohio	180 E Broad St, 16th Floor	Columbus, OH 43215	(614) 466-2655
Oklahoma	State Capitol, Room 122, 2300 N Lincoln Blvd	Oklahoma City, OK 73105	(405) 521-3912
Oregon	900 Court St NE, Capitol Room 136	Salem, OR 97310-0722	(503) 986-1523
Pennsylvania	302 North Office Building, 401 North St	Harrisburg, PA 17120	(717) 787-6458

Rhode Island	148 W River St	Providence, RI 02904-2615	(401) 222-3040
South Carolina	1205 Pendleton St, Ste 525	Columbia, SC 29201	(803) 734-2158
South Dakota	Capitol Building, 500 E Capitol Ave, Ste 204	Pierre, SD 57501-5070	(605) 773-4845
Tennessee	312 Rosa L Parks Ave, 6th Floor, Snodgrass Tower	Nashville, TN 37243-1102	(615) 741-2286
Texas	PO Box 12887	Austin, TX 78711-2887	(512) 463-5555
Utah	160 E 300 South, 2nd Floor	Salt Lake City, UT 84111	(801) 530-4849
Vermont	128 State St	Montpelier, VT 05633-1101	(800) 439-8683
US Virgin Islands	1131 King St, Ste 101	Christiansted, St. Croix, VI 00820	(340) 773-6449
Virginia	PO Box 1475	Richmond, VA 23218	(804) 786-2441
Washington	PO Box 40234	Olympia, WA 98504-0234	(360) 725-0377
West Virginia	State Capitol Building	Charleston, WV 25305	(304) 558-6000

Wisconsin	PO Box 7848	Madison, WI 53707-7848	(608) 266-8888
Wyoming	2020 Carey Ave, Ste 700	Cheyenne, WY 82002-0020	(307) 777-7311
District of Columbia	1350 Pennsylvania Ave NW, Ste 419	Washington, DC 20004	(202) 727-7278
Puerto Rico	Calle San José	San Juan, PR 00901	(787) 722-212

If you are incorporating in a state like Delaware, Florida, Texas, or Arkansas, solid picks for business credit building, expect streamlined online systems, predictable fee structures, and fast processing. These states want your business. On the flip side, states like California will welcome you with a fee schedule so bloated and compliance-heavy that you will need to think twice about incorporating there. It's always been my opinion that the bear on California's state flag was chosen to represent the California Franchise Tax Board. That said, if your business operates in California, **you must** register there regardless. No workaround. Just brace for it, be budget smart, and good luck.

A Word to the Wise on Filing Fees

Fees will change. Sometimes, without any advance warning. The fee today might not be the fee next month. Some states have base filing costs as low as $50, while others tack on licensing fees, business taxes, or annual reports that edge north of $800. And then there is Nevada, where you're shelling out an extra $500 just for the privilege of having a now-mandatory business license. **Read the fine print.** Better yet, call and verify the total cost before sending your paperwork.

That's why this guide includes **the complete Secretary of State contact list**, not just for filing, but for troubleshooting, follow-ups, and getting the inside scoop on whether certain industries or entity types are facing delays or heightened scrutiny.

Naming Your Business: Strategic Language Wins Loans

Now, let's talk about the trap that tanks more business credit applications than anything else: **your company name**. It's not just branding. It's a trigger **for banks, for credit bureaus, for underwriters.** Choose poorly, and your company will be red-flagged and denied for business funding before your application even gets read, and you won't even know why.

The name you choose should work like a key. It should unlock opportunity. That means:

- **Avoid high-risk keywords.** Avoid words like "capital," "investment," "funding," "credit," "leasing," "trust," "real estate," or "financial services." These scream liability, compliance headaches, competition with the bank, and potential risk to banks and business credit underwriters. Remember, you're not building Wall Street, you're building trust.

- **Be descriptive, but neutral.** Go with something like "Precision Supply Group LLC" over "Quick Capital Kings Inc." The former sounds stable. The latter sets off lender alarms.

- **Make it easy to spell, say, and search.** Your name should pass the phone test. If someone hears it once, can they find it online and remember it accurately? If not, revise it immediately.
- **Keep it short and punchy.** You're building a brand, yes, but for credit purposes, the goal is frictionless approval. Simplicity = speed and money.

A good name also helps you avoid unnecessary manual reviews by credit bureaus or lenders. Remember, **algorithms** now do the heavy lifting. They don't "read between the lines." They have been programmed to scan for keywords and categorize risk. Your business name is the first line of code in that equation.

Registering Your Business

Depending on the state where you plan to incorporate and operate, you may need to **foreign register** your corporation with the Secretary of State. This process usually involves filing articles of incorporation (or organization), obtaining a Tax ID (EIN), and registering for state and local taxes.

If securing business funding is your goal, this is not a step to overlook. It also presents a key opportunity: When registering your business, you (if your personal credit is excellent) or your designated Credit Partner/CFO should always be listed as the Registered Agent. Lenders check this information, often without telling you, so it's important to have it aligned with your funding strategy. You want the name of your strongest credit partner up front and center on everything except your business checking account. Publicly linking your CFO's name to the corporation reinforces credibility in the eyes of banks and underwriters and eliminates any questions before they can arise.

Obtaining an Employer Identification Number (EIN)

An EIN is required to open a business bank account, apply for business credit, and file taxes. It's free and easy to obtain through the IRS at this link: https://www.irs.gov/businesses/small-businesses-self-employed/get-an-employer-identification-number

IMPORTANT: Lenders are becoming more thorough. They now have systems in place to cross-check when your EIN was issued. If there is a significant delay between your business formation date and the EIN issuance date—say your LLC was formed in 2021, but your EIN was obtained in 2025—it may raise a red flag. I've seen this happen.

Lenders might wonder:

"Why has this company existed for five years without any financial activity?"

"Could this be a shelf corporation the potential borrower just purchased?" Hmm?"

If they suspect that, **you're out of the running** for funding. The worst part? They may not even give you a chance to explain. Avoid this pitfall by syncing your EIN issuance date with your formation date, or be prepared to offer a confident, reasonable explanation.

Two Critical Timelines You Must Nail

There are two other behind-the-scenes checkpoints that lenders quietly verify during underwriting, and you need to get them right:

1. Build a Professional Website (It's Non-Negotiable)

Before applying for any type of business loan or credit card, you must have a credible, well-structured website. At a minimum, it should include the following five pages:

- **Home**

- **About Us**

- **Products/Services**

- **Our Team**

- **Contact Us**

Additional guidelines:

- Display your **physical business address** (not a residential or Regis office address if your goal is to get bank loans).

- Feature your **name or your CFO's name** prominently throughout, depending on who has the best personal credit.

- List a **business phone number** that is **answered live** Monday through Friday, 9 a.m.–5 p.m.

- **Don't forget the copyright notice.**

   Place this at the bottom left of the home page in small (3–5 pt.) type:
   COPYRIGHT © **[Year of Incorporation]** [Business Name] All Rights Reserved.

You may think it's trivial, but this detail is often quietly used by lenders to verify legitimacy. If unsure, contact the Beverly Hills WFG offices for clarification or consult your legal advisor.

2. **Secure Your Domain Name Early**

Ideally, register your business domain **on the same day** your corporation is formed, or **within 30 days** at most. **This is important**. Certain equipment leasing firms and business lenders **do** check domain registration dates using WHOIS database lookups. An older, timely registered domain looks more credible during underwriting.

Licenses and Permits: Strategy Matters

Based on your industry and local jurisdiction, you may need:

- A general business license

- Zoning permits

- Health permits

- Specialized industry licenses

Here is the strategy: If your personal credit is poor and you're relying on a strong CFO or Credit Partner, **keep your name off licenses and permits**. During the early funding stage, the only place your name should appear is in the business bank accounts. Let your Credit Partner, preferably someone with stellar credit, appear as the public face of the business during the lending process.

Why? Lenders and credit agencies often *assume* the person named on legal documents is the controlling party or majority shareholder. This illusion works in your favor.

Opening Your Business Bank Account

Your choice of business bank is pivotal. A strong banking relationship can jumpstart your credit-building journey.

Here is how to maximize it:

1. Ask to speak with the bank's **business banking specialist**.

2. Share your short-term and long-term credit goals.

3. Open the account with a **substantial deposit** *(the bigger, the better)*.

4. Request a **business credit card** immediately, ideally with a **$15,000 to $50,000** limit.

Many banks are willing to issue a card if your opening deposit is significant and you present your business professionally. This simple, but more often overlooked, first step can set the tone for your entire credit-building strategy.

The Importance of Your Initial Bank Deposit

Your **opening deposit amount** plays a quietly powerful role in shaping how your bank evaluates your business in the future. While rarely discussed publicly, this figure often serves as an internal reference point during later credit evaluations and loan decisions.

Even if you plan to withdraw the funds the next day, making the **largest possible opening deposit** is highly strategic. It sends a message to the bank that you are a serious, well-capitalized operator. On the flip side, if the bank's initial offer disappoints you, **don't rush** to open the account. Shop around. Choose a bank that aligns with your funding goals.

NOTE: Only your name, as Secretary or Treasurer, should appear on your corporation's business bank account.

If you have questions about where to bank (or which banks to avoid), you're welcome to call the Wilshire Financial Group by dialing **1+(888) 383-5318** and asking to speak with a qualified corporate credit advisor. To schedule a one-on-one consult with me personally, you can use the same number.

Business Insurance: Don't Skip It

Depending on your industry and office setup, business insurance may be required to protect against liability and unforeseen risks. If you operate from a physical location, a **basic liability policy** must be a priority. Speak with your insurance agent about the appropriate coverage.

Business Plan: Do You Really Need It?

That depends on your goals.

If you're pursuing a **traditional "full doc" business loan**, plan on applying for an **SBA loan**, or plan on disclosing to the lender that funds will be used for a **startup**, then yes, you will likely need a solid business plan. However, if your goal is to build **corporate credit lines** or secure funding through **credit card stacking, equipment leasing, or private lenders**, a business plan is **not required**. That said, crafting a clear, concise business plan is still a smart move. It can serve as your internal roadmap and help you make strategic decisions, especially when you're just starting out.

A Few Tips:

- Keep it straightforward. Most lenders don't understand your day-to-day operations.

- Focus on **financials** and **forecasts**; this is where lenders pay the most attention.

- Your numbers must align with **D&B industry norms**. To get this right:

- o Find your **SIC code.**

- o Search Dunn & Bradstreet (D&B) for other established businesses in your industry.

- o Purchase a D&B full report on one of those businesses and use that report as your reference and structural financial model.

No time to write your plan? The Wilshire Financial Group offers professional business plan writing services specifically tailored to your business and focused on getting business funding approvals.

Do You Need Employees to Build Business Credit?

Surprisingly, the answer is **no**.

You can build strong business credit without hiring employees. However, if you do plan to hire, you will need to:

- Obtain an **Employer Identification Number (EIN)**.

- Comply with all **federal and state employment laws**.

- Set up reliable **payroll and bookkeeping services**.

Keeping clean payroll records is critical. If needed, reach out to the Wilshire Financial Group's accounting department for support.

Keep Accurate Books from Day One

Setting up **good accounting and bookkeeping systems** is not optional. You will need them to:

- Track income and expenses

- Prepare financial statements

- File accurate tax returns

Again, if this isn't your strong suit, ask your assistant to call **1+(888) 383-5318** and ask my telephone assistant to connect you with the WFG accounting team.

Marketing: Your Business Won't Sell Itself

Once your entity is legally established, the real work begins—**attracting customers**. Key steps include:

- Building a **professional website**

- Networking in your niche or local business community

- Running **targeted ads** (Google, Meta, etc.)

- Leveraging **social media**

If you'd like expert hands-on guidance developing a powerful million-dollar marketing strategy, this is my speciality, and I'm available to help. Contact me, John Garry, directly at **1+(888) 383-5318**

Building a Strong Corporate Credit Foundation

This is what it's all about.

A robust corporate credit profile isn't just for show; it's a **gateway to capital**. It influences everything from interest rates to the confidence of potential lenders and partners.

The Benefits of Solid Corporate Credit:

- Easier access to **working capital**

- **Lower interest rates** on loans and credit cards

- Stronger **vendor and supplier relationships**

- Increased **market credibility**

Lower Interest Rates

A solid corporate credit foundation dramatically improves your chances of securing **lower interest rates**. When lenders evaluate your application, one of the first things they assess is your company's creditworthiness. A strong business credit profile signals lower risk, which in turn qualifies you for more favorable loan terms. Over time, this translates to significant savings, especially on large credit lines or long-term financing agreements.

Increased Business Credibility

Good credit does more than secure capital. It **builds trust**. Vendors, suppliers, and prospective partners view a business with strong credit as reliable, responsible, and safe to work with. This can open doors to better contract terms, more generous trade credit, and collaborative opportunities that wouldn't be available otherwise. In short, strong credit makes your business more attractive and trustworthy.

Steps to Establish and Maintain Strong Business Credit

Here are the key actions you need to take to build a solid foundation:

1. Establish Trade Credit Early

Trade credit is credit extended by vendors or suppliers. It is one of the easiest ways to build your business credit file. Apply for vendor credit accounts early and ensure **on-time or early payments**. Your payment habits, especially with vendors, contribute directly to your credit score.

2. Apply for Business Credit Cards

Vendor-specific and general-purpose business credit cards are relatively easy to obtain and often **do not require a personal guarantor.** Use them responsibly and pay them off promptly to build your payment history.

3. Monitor Business Credit Reports

Regularly review your **Experian Business Report**, among others, to ensure all information is accurate. Errors, even minor ones, can drag down your score and prevent you from qualifying for funding. Early detection allows for timely dispute and correction.

4. Incorporate Your Business

Creating a legal corporate entity establishes a clear separation between personal and business finances, which is essential for building credit. If your target is securing **$250,000 to $1,000,000+** in business funding, the **C corporation** structure should be your preferred path.

Let's break down why.

Why a "C" Corporation Is Ideal for Funding

When your goal is **large credit lines**, your business structure matters a lot to prospective lenders.

"C" Corporations = "Credit & Cash"
"S" Corporations = "Small Business"

Key Advantages of a "C" Corporation:

- **Higher Credit Limits:** C corporations are eligible for larger lines of business credit than LLCs or S-corps.

- **Increased Credibility:** Banks and lenders perceive C corporations as business corporations, more established, professional, and stable.

- **Limited Liability:** Shareholders' personal assets are shielded unless a personal guarantee is made.

- **Tax Benefits:** C corporations are separate taxable entities, allowing for strategic reinvestment of profits and unique tax deductions.

- **Perpetual Existence:** The company continues to operate even if ownership changes.

- **Capital Raising:** The ability to issue stock gives C corporations a massive advantage when seeking growth capital.

While forming a C corporation from scratch is powerful, remember it requires time, **up to three years**, before you will qualify for major funding.

The Fast-Track: Purchasing a Seasoned Corporation

If waiting three years isn't realistic, there is an accelerated route: **acquiring a seasoned, aged corporation**.

The Wilshire Financial Group offers **fully established entities**, 3+ years old, complete with:

- Corporate kits, seals, and IRS-issued EIN numbers

- Built-for-you business websites and solid domain names

- Three (3) professional and strategic business email accounts

- Properly maintained minutes and legal records

- Historical tax filings where applicable
- Structured and engineered business-specific corporations to meet the **current lender guidelines**

Each WFG corporation comes with a **money-back guarantee** should it fail to qualify for funding due to any issue with the company itself.

Other Benefits:

- Immediate funding potential
- Stronger credit profile out of the gate
- Higher approval odds for six-figure funding
- Potential tax advantages
- Lower personal liability

If your objective is to raise between **$250,000 and $1,000,000+ in under 9 months**, purchasing a seasoned corporation is your smartest play.

You can explore available options online by going to https://wilshirefinancialservices.com or calling **1+(888) 383-5318** Monday through Friday between 9:00 a.m. and 5:00 p.m. PST to speak directly with an experienced business advisor.

Seamless Mergers with No Red Flags

Planning to merge your current business into a seasoned corporation? Wilshire Financial Group's expert team can handle the entire process **without triggering any " financial stress alerts"** or making any waves on your business credit reports.

This is crucial, as such alerts can automatically disqualify you from funding for up to six months.

When you work with WFG, your seasoned company:

- Will be matched to your SIC code and business model

- Can be merged with your existing business operations quickly, cleanly, and quietly

- Comes with a **no-risk guarantee** against funding rejection

- Includes **complimentary round-trip airfare** to our Beverly Hills office, should you request, for an in-person consultation

Meeting face-to-face ensures your strategy is tailored specifically to your business goals, financial profile, and industry.

Disadvantages of Forming a C Corporation

While C corporations offer numerous advantages, particularly for raising significant business funding, they also come with certain tradeoffs that are important to consider.

1. Double Taxation

Perhaps the most commonly cited downside is **double taxation**. This means corporate profits are taxed twice: once at the corporate level and again when dividends and profits are distributed to shareholders. For some, this might seem burdensome.

However, in this author's professional opinion, double taxation is a **small price to pay** for the benefits a C corporation provides, especially if your primary goal is securing **maximum corporate credit and funding potential**. If you do not already have a skilled business tax advisor, I strongly recommend contacting the Wilshire Financial Group in Beverly Hills, California. Call us toll-free at **1+(888) 383-5318,** ask to be transferred to one of our Wilshire Group business accountants or our in-house IRS Enrolled Agent, or even to schedule a consultation with a California-licensed tax attorney.

2. Complex Formation and Operation

C corporations involve more paperwork and legal requirements than LLCs or sole proprietorships. This includes:

- Filing articles of incorporation

- Drafting bylaws

- Holding regular shareholder and board meetings

- Complying with detailed state and federal reporting requirements

However, this complexity should not be viewed as a roadblock, especially if your objective is to qualify immediately for business credit. If you prefer to avoid the paperwork altogether, consider **purchasing a seasoned, three-year-old C corporation** from the Wilshire Financial Group or another reputable source. The right firm can handle all these steps for you.

3. Increased Regulation

C corporations face more regulatory scrutiny. This includes compliance with tax laws, securities regulations, and formal recordkeeping. Fortunately, if you're running a legitimate business and have secured the appropriate licenses, **these obligations should not present any major issues**.

4. Limited Flexibility

C corporations are bound by strict formalities and operating procedures, making them less nimble than other entity types. If your business needs to pivot quickly or make structural changes, you may encounter more red tape. Still, the tradeoff is often worth it for companies pursuing large-scale growth.

5. Upfront and Ongoing Costs

Operating a C corporation can be more expensive. Between legal fees, compliance filings, and required maintenance, costs can add up. That said, if your goal is to **secure meaningful business funding**, these upfront expenses should be viewed as **an investment** with substantial long-term returns.

Before forming or purchasing a C corporation, **weigh the pros and cons carefully**, and consult with your legal or financial advisor. And one more thing I strongly advise from experience, if you're married, **don't forget to run this by your spouse**!

Recap: Why Corporate Credit Matters

Building a **strong corporate credit foundation** is one of the most valuable moves a business owner can make.

Here is why:

- **Access to Financing**

   Businesses with solid credit profiles are more likely to be approved for loans, credit lines, equipment leases, and working capital. Credit history is often the **first filter** lenders use to determine eligibility.

- **Improved Loan Terms**

  Not only are approvals easier, but the terms improve dramatically. That means lower interest rates, better repayment periods, and easier access to capital when opportunities arise.

- **Stronger Cash Flow**

  With access to financing, your company can fund operations, manage payroll, stock inventory, and invest in growth without interrupting your cash reserves. Good credit also improves vendor relationships, often allowing for:

  - Longer payment windows

  - Early-payment discounts

  - Reduced upfront costs

- **Separation of Personal and Business Credit**

A solid corporate credit profile protects your personal credit and assets. This legal separation shields you in the event of business downturns or liability issues. In other words, your **personal credit rating remains intact**, and your excellent corporate credit profile **effectively doubles your financial leverage**.

Let me be perfectly clear: **Corporate credit is a game-changer**. It opens doors. It gives you leverage. It gives your business room to breathe and grow. Whether you build your company from scratch or purchase a ready-made seasoned corporation, the result is the same:

a new business identity, a new credit profile, and access to financial tools that can dramatically accelerate your path to success.

The Difference Between a D/B/A., a Limited Liability Company, and a Corporation

Choosing the right legal structure for your business is one of the most important decisions you will make as an entrepreneur. Whether you're launching a small operation or planning to build a national brand, the structure you select will directly affect your personal liability, taxes, funding opportunities, and long-term flexibility.

What Is a D/B/A?

A **d/b/a** (Doing Business As) allows an individual or business to operate under a name other than their legal name. It is not a separate legal entity, and it provides no liability protection. Sole proprietors or partnerships commonly use a d/b/a when they wish to brand their business under a different name from their own.

Key point: A d/b/a does not separate personal and business liabilities. The owner remains personally responsible for all debts, obligations, and legal actions.

What Is a Limited Liability Company (LLC)?

An **LLC** is a flexible business structure that offers limited liability protection to its owners, known as "members." The LLC is a separate legal entity from its owners, which means that members' personal assets are protected from the business's debts and legal liabilities.

LLCs can elect to be taxed as:

- A sole proprietorship (if single-member)

- A partnership (if multi-member)

- A corporation (if they choose to be taxed that way)

This makes the LLC a highly flexible structure, especially attractive to startups and small business owners looking for both protection and simplicity.

What Is a Corporation?

A **corporation** is a separate legal entity that also offers limited liability protection, but it operates under a more formal management and regulatory structure. Corporations are owned by **shareholders**, managed by a **board of directors**, and operated by appointed **officers**.

Corporations can be taxed as:

- A **C corporation**, where the business is taxed separately from the owners (with potential double taxation on dividends)

- An **S corporation**, where profits pass through to shareholders to avoid double taxation (subject to eligibility criteria)

Comparison Overview

Feature	d/b/a	LLC	Corporation
Liability Protection	None	Yes	Yes

Legal Entity Status	Not separate	Separate	Separate
Tax Flexibility	None—taxed personally	Flexible	C or S Corp election
Ownership	Individual or partners	Unlimited members	Unlimited shareholders
Management	Owner-managed	Member-managed or manager-managed	Board of directors & officers
Ease of Formation	Easiest	Moderate	Most complex
Ideal for	Simple, small businesses	Startups, growing small businesses	Growth-focused, high-capital ventures

Final Considerations

The decision between operating as a d/b/a, LLC, or corporation should align with your:

- **Liability risk** (Do you want your personal assets protected?)

- **Tax strategy**

- **Desire to raise funding**

- **Short- and long-term growth plans**

If you're building a business with serious funding needs or long-term scalability in mind, forming an LLC or corporation will almost always serve you better than a d/b/a. However, the nuances of each structure and how they interact with your industry, state laws, and personal financial situation make professional consultation essential.

Before moving forward, I would suggest consulting a business attorney or licensed tax advisor. The right foundation could save you from costly restructuring and protect your assets as your company grows.

Chapter 4

Obtaining Necessary Business Licenses and Permits

"I may walk slowly, but I never walk backwards."

—Abraham Lincoln

Launching a business is more than choosing a name and filing paperwork; it's about ensuring your business operates legally and is properly authorized by your city, county, or state. Whether you're running a sole proprietorship under a d/b/a, managing an LLC, or steering a full-fledged corporation, obtaining the right licenses and permits is non-negotiable.

The Business License

A business license grants you legal permission to operate in a specific municipality. Nearly every city and county across the country requires one, largely to ensure they can track your operations and collect taxes appropriately.

For a real education, visit Beverly Hills City Hall and inform them you'd like to open a business there. You will walk away with more paperwork, regulations, and requirements than you thought possible, along with a full understanding of how complicated a local system can truly be. Consider it an advanced course in municipal compliance. You will walk away with a brand-new respect for deciding to do business in your hometown.

Here is the truth: Beverly Hills is one of the most demanding places in the US to start a business, particularly if it's your first. If you value your time, you may consider launching your venture elsewhere.

For the rest of the country, obtaining a basic business license usually just requires a smile and submission of your d/b/a, LLC articles, or incorporation documents.

Zoning Permit

Zoning permits authorize you to conduct a specific type of business at a particular address. Every city has its own zoning code that limits what type of activity is allowed where. Whether you're a d/b/a, LLC, or corporation, you will need to confirm your business type is permitted at your desired location. If not, you may need to apply for a zoning variance, an often time-consuming and unpredictable process.

Sales Tax Permit

If your business involves selling goods, or in some states, taxable services, you will need a sales tax permit. This allows you to collect sales tax on behalf of your state and remit it accordingly. The application process is usually straightforward and can be completed online through your state's department of revenue.

Health Permit

Businesses involved in food service or health-related services must obtain a health permit. These permits are issued by your local or county health department and require an inspection to ensure compliance with sanitation and health codes. This applies to all business types, d/b/a, LLC, or corporation.

Pro tip: Don't forget to wash your hands before that inspection.

Building Permit

Planning to build out or renovate a commercial space? You will likely need a building permit from the city's building department. This applies whether you're adding walls, installing equipment, or updating plumbing and electrical systems. Operating without a permit could result in hefty fines, forced removal of work, or even a business shutdown.

Sign Permit

A sign permit gives you the green light to install exterior signage on your business property. Municipalities want to regulate the size, lighting, and placement of signage to maintain aesthetics and safety. You will need to submit a proposed design to your local zoning or planning department for approval.

Professional License

Certain professions, such as law, accounting, architecture, cosmetology, and medical services, require individual practitioners to hold a professional license. These are issued by state licensing boards and often require exams, continuing education, and annual renewals. If you're operating in a regulated industry, this license is as vital as your business registration.

The specific licenses and permits required for your business will depend on three things:

- **Your business structure (d/b/a, LLC, or corporation)**

- **Your location**

- **Your industry**

Failing to secure the appropriate licenses can result in fines, penalties, or even the forced closure of your business. Take the time to check with your city hall, county clerk's office, and state licensing boards. When in doubt, consult a local business attorney or licensing consultant.

Next up: we'll explore how to position your business for maximum credibility and funding power through smart compliance steps.

Chapter 5

Business-Friendly Banks and the Not-So-Friendly

"If everything isn't black and white, I say, why the hell not?"

—John Wayne

The Importance of Opening a Separate Business Bank Account

Opening a dedicated business bank account is essential to properly separating your business and personal finances. This distinction simplifies income and expense tracking, streamlines tax filing, and safeguards your personal assets in the event of legal actions involving your business, provided your financial records are well-maintained.

Builds Business Credit

A separate business bank account is instrumental in establishing and growing your company's credit profile. If you plan to apply for loans, lease equipment or vehicles, or acquire credit cards, having strong business credit will lead to better loan terms, reduced interest rates, and higher credit limits.

Provides Clear Financial Records

Accurate financial records are easier to maintain with a standalone business account. These records will prove invaluable for preparing financial statements, managing taxes, and presenting your business to lenders, investors, or other stakeholders.

Offers Business-Friendly Services

Most banks offer specialized services for businesses, such as payroll processing, merchant accounts, and digital banking tools. These services help streamline operations and save time. Many also provide access to credit cards, lines of credit, and other financial products tailored to business needs.

Top Business-Friendly Banks for New Accounts

U.S. Bank

With nearly two decades of experience in corporate credit building, I've guided hundreds of clients in securing millions in small business loans. Of all the options available today, US Bank remains my top recommendation for business banking.

US Bank stands out as one of the few institutions still allowing entrepreneurs to open new business checking and savings accounts online. They offer a comprehensive suite of business banking services, including credit cards, lines of credit, and unsecured loans. Their team of business bankers provides valuable support for account management and long-term planning.

New business clients often walk away with a $30,000+ business credit card line upon opening both checking and merchant accounts. Their low- or no-fee online platform is efficient, and after 40+ years of banking with US Bank myself, I can vouch for their consistency and customer support.

Chase Bank for Business

Chase is another strong contender, offering business credit cards, loans with sizable limits, and dedicated support for business customers. I've opened multiple accounts with Chase and have consistently found their team to be professional and genuinely interested in supporting small business success.

However, it's worth noting that Chase increasingly values relationship banking. They prefer customers who consolidate both personal and business finances with them. If you're considering Chase, start by booking a meeting with a business loan officer. Present your business goals and outline how you envision their support fitting into your strategy. Then, open:

- A business checking account (with the largest deposit possible)

- A business savings account

- Both personal checking and savings accounts

Before leaving, request a business credit card application. Take it home, complete it, and return it in person within two business days to the officer you met initially. If they're unavailable, ask when they'll be back and deliver the application directly to them. This kind of personal follow-up can go a long way toward building a successful banking relationship.

CoAmerica Bank

CoAmerica offers highly business-friendly services, including generous credit cards, lines of credit, and term loans. They also maintain a strong, responsive team of business bankers dedicated to helping with account management and loan applications.

One particular CoAmerica branch has even sent several of its top business loan specialists to our Beverly Hills offices to participate in our weekend business credit seminars. Many attendees left those events with their small business loan applications already submitted, and in several cases, funding secured. I've collected some truly entertaining stories from those weekends, but I'll save those for another time.

Capital One

Capital One provides a full range of services for small businesses, including credit cards, lines of credit, and loans. Their digital banking platform is streamlined and user-friendly, allowing for easy account management and financial tracking from virtually anywhere.

Mechanics Bank

Mechanics Bank stands out for small businesses focused on real estate. They provide credit cards, flexible business lines, and financing for commercial acquisitions, residential rehab projects, multi-family properties, and new construction. Their online banking tools are reliable, and they offer letters of credit as well, ideal for developers and real estate entrepreneurs.

Valley Bank

Valley National Bancorp, operating as Valley Bank, is headquartered in Morristown, New Jersey, and holds approximately

$64 billion in assets. Over the years, we at Wilshire Financial have had excellent success placing our small business clients with Valley.

With more than 200 branches and commercial offices across the US, Valley Bank is easy to access. They employ more than 3,800 professionals who serve clients in commercial, industrial, healthcare, nonprofit, real estate, and government sectors. If you're looking for a reliable partner with scale and specialized lending options, they deserve serious consideration.

Choose Carefully

Opening a dedicated business bank account is one of the most important steps you will take toward responsible financial management and building corporate credit. Take your time. Shop around. Each bank offers a different mix of products, customer service quality, and underwriting leniency. Match their strengths to your business's location, structure, and financial needs.

The S**t List: The Not-So-Friendly Bank

Only one bank has earned a spot on my *"Do Not Recommend"* list.

Years ago, I would've told you it was the best small business lender bank in the game. Our point of contact, let's call her Mary, handled hundreds of client referrals at their Beverly Hills and Sunset locations. It was common for those clients to leave the same day with newly opened checking accounts and pre-approved business credit cards. Mary was exceptional—professional and sharp—and she truly understood the needs of entrepreneurs.

Then she got promoted.

From there, this bank's customer service plummeted. Internal policies became rigid, support dried up, and the welcoming environment turned into a bureaucratic obstacle course.

To this day, whenever someone asks me about that bank, my mind jumps to a line from *Apocalypse Now*, Marlon Brando's haunted whisper as Colonel Kurtz: *"The horror … I've seen the horror …"*

If you're wondering which bank I'm talking about, don't stress, we won't send you there. That chapter is closed.

Chapter 6

Vendor Credit

"All our dreams can come true if we have the courage to pursue them."

—Walt Disney

Establishing Trade Credit with Vendors

Trade credit is a form of short-term financing that allows businesses to purchase goods and services from vendors without having to pay up front. Instead, payment is deferred, usually within 30, 60, or 90 days, helping to preserve cash flow and streamline operations.

For startups and newer businesses, trade credit is especially valuable. It enables day-to-day purchasing without draining cash reserves, and, just as importantly, it contributes to the development of a business credit profile. Timely payments to vendors are reported to commercial credit bureaus, establishing a positive history that strengthens your credibility with future lenders and suppliers.

Benefits of Vendor Credit Accounts

Opening vendor credit accounts early in your business journey provides several key advantages:

- **Preserves Cash Flow**: By not paying immediately, you retain more working capital to manage other expenses or invest in growth.

- **Builds Business Credit**: Responsible usage and on-time payments build your company's credit history and improve credit scores.

- **Demonstrates Credibility**: Vendors and lenders view an active, well-managed trade credit portfolio as a sign of financial responsibility.

- **Improves Purchasing Power**: As your credit history grows, so does your access to higher limits and better payment terms.

Ten Vendor Accounts That Offer Net- 30 Terms, No Personal Guarantee Required

Each of the vendors below offers net-30 terms to new businesses without requiring a personal guarantee. That means you can begin building business credit without putting your personal credit on the line:

1. **Uline**

   A top supplier of shipping, packaging, and industrial materials. Uline is an ideal vendor for startups needing warehouse or office supply essentials. They offer net-30 terms with no personal guarantee.

2. **Grainger**

   One of the largest industrial supply companies in the US, Grainger is a powerhouse for tools, maintenance equipment, and facility management items. Net-30 terms are available to new businesses.

3. Quill

A go-to resource for office supplies, Quill is known for issuing net-30 vendor credit accounts quickly. They report regularly to commercial credit bureaus, making them a prime choice for businesses serious about building credit.

4. Global Industrial

Specializing in commercial and industrial equipment, Global Industrial offers net-30 payment terms without a personal guarantee. They cater to businesses across many sectors.

5. Amsterdam Printing

Perfect for custom branding, Amsterdam Printing offers promotional materials and marketing products. They extend net-30 accounts to new businesses and are known for customer-friendly service.

6. Viking

An office supply vendor offering a wide selection of furniture, stationery, and electronics. Viking supports net-30 payment terms for businesses with no PG required.

7. Monoprice

Known for affordable electronics, cables, and accessories, Monoprice is a smart option for tech-based startups. They provide net-30 terms to qualifying new businesses.

8. MSC Industrial Supply

MSC delivers a broad array of tools, safety gear, and industrial equipment. Their net-30 account offering is well-suited for manufacturing or construction-related businesses.

9. Seton

A niche vendor specializing in safety signs, labeling systems, and compliance identification products. They offer net-30 terms to new business accounts.

10. Wilshire Financial Group Inc.

Unlike traditional vendors, Wilshire Financial Group Inc. provides corporate structuring services, professional websites, SEO engineering, accounting, and business financial products. They extend payment terms and financing to new businesses with no personal guarantee, reporting monthly to all major business credit bureaus.

Chapter 7

Applying for Secured Business Credit

"Some people you can't teach. They just won't listen. They think they know everything. However, most don't know the difference between their ass and their elbow. But that's a good thing because these people would be very dangerous with a little bit of knowledge."

—John Garry

Applying for Secured Business Credit

Establishing business credit takes patience, precision, and a bit of strategic thinking. Applying for a secured business credit card is one avenue to help build or strengthen your business's credit profile, but it must be approached with care and preparation.

Step 1: Research the Right Card

Begin by researching secured business credit cards and comparing their features, fees, and benefits. Look for a card with low annual fees, a competitive interest rate, and reward programs that align with your business spending. Not all cards are created equal; take time to find the right fit.

Step 2: Don't Go Off Half-Cocked—Know Your Credit Score

Before applying, check your personal and business credit scores. Many secured cards have minimum credit score requirements. Several credit bureaus and services offer free access to your current score, so use them to gauge where you stand.

Step 3: Get Your Act Together, Gather Required Documents

You will need to present a complete financial picture when applying. Be sure to have the following documents ready:

- Your business's Tax ID (EIN)

- A valid and current business license

- At least three months of business bank statements

- The past two years of both state and federal business tax returns

- Recent financial statements (if available)

Submitting an incomplete application wastes your time and raises red flags. Have your documentation in order.

Step 4: Choose Your Deposit Amount Wisely

A secured business credit card requires a cash deposit, typically equal to your requested credit limit. The larger the deposit, the higher your starting credit line. Consider how much you're willing and able to tie up as collateral. Most banks allow deposits via wire transfer, check, or direct bank draft.

Step 5: Complete the Application Carefully

Accuracy is crucial. Use your **physical** business address (not a Post Office Box), give your **correct and listed 411 telephone**

number, and never attempt to manipulate your Social Security number or use false business data. There is no room for games here. One misstep, especially anything flagged as potential fraud, can derail your credit-building journey.

Step 6: Submit Strategically, Avoid Online Portals

Although many banks offer online applications, resist the temptation. These forms are first scanned by automated systems, not humans, and data shows that over **62 percent** of online applications are denied outright. Instead, request a **paper application** by phone or in person. Submit it directly to a banker who can advocate for your approval. The effort is well worth it.

Step 7: Wait for the Decision, Patiently

After submission, please give it time. Some approvals are issued in hours; others take several days. Lenders may request follow-up documents or ask questions to verify your application. Avoid the urge to jump ship and apply elsewhere in the meantime.

Important: Many major banks now use the same underwriting companies to process business credit applications. If you apply to multiple institutions at once, you're essentially resubmitting to the same evaluator, raising red flags and likely triggering multiple denials. The days of shotgun applications or "daisy-chaining" banks are gone.

Pro Tip:

Submit one application at a time. Follow up, wait for the outcome, and proceed based on feedback.

Step 8: Fund Your Deposit Promptly

Once approved, you will need to fund the deposit quickly to activate the account. This is often done via bank transfer or check. Don't delay: Funding late can delay or even cancel the approval.

Step 9: Activate and Begin Using Your Card

Upon confirmation of your deposit, the card will be mailed to you. Follow the issuer's instructions to activate the card, usually online or by phone. Once activated, begin using it for modest, routine business expenses. Pay your balance on time, or better yet, early, to start building strong business credit immediately.

Use Your Cards Responsibly!

Once your secured business credit card is activated, begin using it to cover essential business purchases. However, use it wisely. Charge only what your business can comfortably repay, and always pay your balance in full, not just the minimum, and pay on time. Early or full payments every month will steadily build your business credit profile.

If you manage the card responsibly and use it regularly, you should see results quickly. After **90 days** of consistent use and full repayment, reach out to the issuing lender and request the following:

- An **increase in your credit limit**

- A **reduction in your interest rate**

- **The release of the secured deposit requirement**

Most lenders won't hesitate to increase your limit or reduce your rate if you've proven to be a responsible borrower. However, most will not release the secured balance or personal guarantee until they've reviewed a full 12-month repayment history, not just with them, but across all of your business credit accounts.

Use this as your guiding principle: Charge up to the limit, pay it off in full by the due date, and maintain that discipline. Every 90 days, make the same call, ask for better terms. Persistent, responsible borrowers often see steady improvements in their credit capacity over the first year.

Critical Warning

Never default on your payments, especially within the first year. And do **not** misuse the funds. Using loan or credit proceeds for personal items, vacations, cars, jewelry, payroll, or entertainment unrelated to business can be potentially considered loan fraud or misappropriation of funds. If your lender suspects that you had no genuine intent to repay, they begin looking into your business, and you risk being flagged for fraud. In many states, loan fraud is a felony offense. Enough said. You get the message: Treat your business credit like gold.

Chapter 8

The 10 Costliest Mistakes Entrepreneurs Make When Applying for Business Funding

"The difference between stupidity and genius is that genius has its limits."

—**Albert Einstein**

Some lessons in business come gently. Others come with a punch to the gut, and you don't forget them for the rest of your life. When it comes to applying for business credit, most owners don't get a gentle introduction; they get the punch. I've been involved in the corporate credit world for over five decades, and I've seen every version of the same story more times than I can count. A business owner walks in full of confidence, thinking they've done everything right, and then they walk out of the bank rubbing the sting from a rejection they never saw coming.

The truth is simple: Most people make the same mistakes. They don't know how business credit actually works. They don't know what lenders are really looking for. And worst of all, they don't know how unforgiving the banking system can be when you're unprepared. These mistakes aren't minor paperwork errors; they're landmines. Step on one, and the bank won't just deny your application; they might quietly "flag" your company. When that happens, you can forget walking into any bank for the next six to twelve months. You will get turned down everywhere, usually without an explanation. That's why this chapter matters.

Here are the **10 biggest mistakes business owners make when applying for business credit**, and every one of them is based on real people, real companies, and real consequences. I either made these mistakes myself in the early years or spent years helping clients dig themselves out after they made them. Avoiding them doesn't require genius. It requires awareness, preparation, and a willingness to follow a process even when your instincts want to take shortcuts.

Let me be clear about something upfront: This list isn't a complete step-by-step loan blueprint. I'll cover that later. What I'm giving you here is the foundation, the list of things you absolutely cannot get wrong. Miss just one, and all the hard work you put into forming your business, building your credit, and preparing your application can go straight down the drain.

Business credit isn't rocket science, but it *is* precision work. There are more moving parts than most people expect, and lenders today are far more cautious than lenders from 20 or 30 years ago. If you want money, real money, not the token $2,500 or $5,000 starter credit cards banks throw at amateurs, then you have to do it right from the beginning. The banks have shifted their underwriting, their screening process, and their approval systems. They have computer programs that can connect dots most people don't even know exist. A home address, a missing phone listing, a suspended corporation, a website with broken links, any one of these can send your application to the denial pile faster than you can say, "What happened?"

And once you're in that denial pile? You stay there for months.

Before you dive into the mistakes, it helps to understand how people learn and internalize new information. I teach this to every client because knowing the steps helps you avoid panicking, rushing, or skipping ahead. There are four stages everyone moves through when learning something new, and business credit is no exception.

Stage 1: Unconscious Incompetence

This is where you don't know what you don't know. Most early mistakes are born right here. You fill out an application without understanding the signals you're sending to the lender. You operate under a d/b/a, thinking it's "good enough." You call your home office your "corporate headquarters." You think lenders will overlook it because you're a nice person and you have "great energy." They won't.

Stage 2: Conscious Incompetence

This is the moment it clicks. You finally realize you *don't know* what you're doing. It's humbling and uncomfortable, but it's also the turning point. This is when people start asking questions, seeking help, and trying to understand the process instead of guessing their way through it. Most clients who come to me arrive at this stage after one or two failed applications.

Stage 3: Conscious Competence

Here, you know what to do, but you still have to think about it. You move carefully. You ask an expert when something feels off. You double-check details. You stop cutting corners. This is the stage where money finally starts becoming available.

Stage 4: Unconscious Competence

This is where it becomes second nature, automatic. You understand how lenders think. You know the order of operations. You can spot mistakes instantly. You navigate the system with the confidence of experience. Once you reach this stage, the world truly does open up. No more fear of rejection and no more guessing. No more spinning your wheels.

And let me tell you something: Reaching this stage is no accident. It comes from absorbing the information, using it correctly, and taking the business loan lending process seriously.

By the time you finish this chapter, and once you learn the step-by-step system I lay out later in the book, you will move through the first three stages. The fourth stage comes only through repetition and real-world action. But once you reach it? You will never again fear a bank loan officer. You will never walk into an application blind. And you will never again feel powerless in the world of business funding.

Now that you've got the framework, let's walk through the mistakes—the same mistakes that cost people tens of thousands, sometimes millions—simply because they didn't know better.

Once you understand how easily a business can get flagged and how quickly the banks can shut the door, the first five mistakes will make perfect sense. These aren't abstract ideas or technical oversights. They are simple, real-world missteps that instantly tell a lender, "This business isn't ready, and this applicant doesn't understand how commercial credit works." Once that message is sent, it's nearly impossible to undo.

Let's break down the first five mistakes, the ones that derail most business owners before the loan officer even reads the second page of their application.

Mistake #1: Not Being Incorporated

You would not believe how many business owners sink their chances before they even start. They walk in with a d/b/a, "doing business as," thinking it's a business structure. It's not. It's a nickname. That's all it is. A d/b/a might work fine for a neighborhood dog walker or someone selling crafts at weekend markets, but banks see it for what it is: a tiny, fragile, one-person operation with no legal backbone.

Here is the reality:

Banks approve corporations faster. They approve higher limits. They trust incorporated businesses more.

Why? Because incorporation signals seriousness, structure, and accountability; a corporation has officers, bylaws, a board, corporate records, and an actual legal presence. A d/b/a has a form filed at the county office and a shoebox full of receipts.

If you walk into any bank with a d/b/a, they might smile at you, but behind the scenes, their system is already stamping your application with "small business, low limit." Best case? A starter card with a tiny credit line. Worst case? Rejection.

In all my years in this field, I have never seen a d/b/a outperform a properly structured corporation. Incorporation is step number one. Without it, every door stays half-closed.

Mistake #2: Having a Corporation That's Too New

This one surprises people. They think, "But I formed my company legally. Why does age matter?"

Because in the eyes of the banking world, a new corporation is a risk. It has no history, no track record, no demonstrated stability. Banks interpret anything under three years old exactly the same way you'd react if someone tried to hand you their newborn and asked you to trust it to run your house for the weekend.

Doesn't matter how good the business idea is. Doesn't matter how strong your intentions are. Lenders want seasoning. They want to know your experience.

That's why I tell clients, and why I've repeated it to thousands of entrepreneurs over the years, **if you want serious funding fast, and you don't have time to wait for three years, buy a seasoned corporation.** There are companies that specialize in creating, maintaining, and aging corporate structures so that when you acquire them, they instantly give you the credibility of a business with years behind it.

Bank computers will reject your loan application simply based on the age of your company.

You can fight this fact and give it a try. You will be turned down. Or, save time, accept it, acquire an aged corporation, and position yourself for fast approval.

Mistake #3: Your Corporation Is Suspended or Not in Good Standing

You'd be shocked at how many people don't know the status of their own corporation. They assume everything is fine … until a lender checks. And trust me, the lender will check immediately.

Banks search your corporation in seconds, faster than you can blink.

If they see *"Suspended," "Not Active," "Delinquent,"* or *"Not in Good Standing,"* your application will be denied shortly after you finish shaking the banker's hand.

A corporation can get suspended for:

- unpaid state franchise taxes

- unpaid registered agent fees

- missing annual reports

- failing to maintain proper filings

- no foreign registration

The fix is simple: keep the lights on. Pay your fees. Renew your filings. Know your corporate status like you know your own name.

If your corporation has ever been suspended for longer than six months, that history may follow you. Some lenders won't touch a corporation that has a long suspension on record. These systems remember everything.

If you want approval, your business must be clean on paper.

Mistake #4: Not Registering Your Corporation to Do Business in Your State

Another common mistake happens when business owners form their corporation in Nevada, Wyoming, or Delaware because someone told them it "looks better" or "protects assets."

Nothing wrong with forming in those states, but you still must **register your corporation as a foreign entity in the state where you actually operate.**

If you don't?

The lender will see a mismatch, and that mismatch sends up a bright red flag. In many states, you cannot even open up a business checking account unless your company is registered in that state to do business.

Is a Nevada corporation operating in Ohio without registering in Ohio?

Rejection.

A Wyoming LLC operating in Florida without registration?

Rejection.

This is one of the fastest deal-killers in the book.

The solution?

If your corporation was formed in a state other than the one in which you are operating, register it also in your state. It's fast, cheap, and necessary. Don't skip this. The bank won't overlook it.

Mistake #5: No Brick-and-Mortar Business Address

This one ruins more applications than almost anything else. People want to save money, so they use their home address, a PO Box, a UPS mailbox, or a virtual office in a Regis suite. They think no one will notice.

The banks notice immediately.

Every lender has software that ranks the type of address on your application. Home address? Instant downgrade. Virtual office? High-risk profile. Shared commercial space? It can be potentially contaminated by another tenant's bad banking history. Proceed with caution and do your homework before you sign the lease. Know the tenants you plan to occupy the office space with.

Here is what most people don't know:

Using a flagged address can significantly reduce your chances of being funded, even if you personally did everything correctly.

If someone else at that same address has unpaid loans, closed accounts, overdraft histories, or ChexSystems issues, the address becomes radioactive. The bank won't touch it, and you will be denied with no explanation.

What's the alternative?

Find a clean, legitimate business district address. Not expensive space, just credible space. Even renting a small private office or paying a local professional for mail-handling services can give your business everything the lender wants to see. The bank wants to know your business is real, stable, and tied to a legitimate commercial location. Don't give them any reason to doubt you.

By the time a business owner reaches Mistake #6, the damage is often already done. The lender has formed an opinion, the underwriter has quietly downgraded the file, and the system is already leaning toward a denial. Yet these next three mistakes are the ones that push most applications off the cliff entirely. They seem small. They seem harmless. But they matter more than most people realize.

These mistakes tell the lender, "This applicant hasn't prepared, hasn't researched, and isn't serious." In the commercial lending world, that's enough to end the conversation before it even begins.

Let's break down Mistakes 6 through 8.

Mistake #6: No Business Telephone Number (and No 411 Listing)

If you walk into a lender's office without a legitimate business telephone number, you've already failed the first credibility test.

Banks expect a real business to have:

- a dedicated business phone number

- a live, professional answer during business hours

- a 411-directory listing

- no background noise, chaos, or residential signals

This isn't about old-fashioned formality; it's about verification. Lenders want to know three things immediately:

1. **Are you a real business?**
   A business with no 411 listing or no dedicated number looks unstable.

2. **Are you reachable?**
   Underwriters often make verification calls. If they hear dogs barking, TVs blaring, or a casual greeting, it signals risk.

3. **Do you operate like a legitimate business?**
   A Monday-to-Friday, 9-to-5, professionally answered phone line shows structure.

Most first-time applicants fail this test because they try to run everything from their cell phone. That may work for personal convenience, but it does not work for lenders.

A serious business has a serious telephone solution.

RingCentral is one of the best options because it offers:

- toll-free numbers

- live answering services

- forwarding features

- voicemail-to-email

- and, importantly, compatibility with 411 listings

Business loan officers appreciate this because it feels legitimate. It's simple. It checks every verification box. It's exactly what banks expect to see.

If your phone setup looks like a side hustle, your application will be treated like one.

Mistake #7: No Business Website (or a Website That You Built Last Night)

This one is new in the lending world, but it's now one of the most important credibility checkpoints. A decade ago, lenders didn't care whether you had a website. Today, it's non-negotiable.

Every lender, from major banks to small business credit providers, uses your website as a digital fingerprint. They expect your business to have:

- a functioning, modern website

- at least three pages (Home, About, Contact at minimum), though five is preferred

- working links

- correct business information

- matching address, matching phone numbers, matching entity details

If your website is missing, broken, unfinished, outdated, or inconsistent with your application, the underwriter assumes:

- Your business is too new.

- Your business is unstable.

- Your business is not legitimate.

And once that assumption is made, the application goes downhill fast.

Remember: Lenders are working with thousands of applicants. They must be able to sort legitimate companies from risky ones quickly. A clean, accurate, professional website is one of the fastest ways to prove credibility.

Another common mistake is hiring a cheap web developer who throws together a template with broken links or placeholder text. Lenders see it instantly. You might not notice the mistakes, but the underwriter definitely will.

A website must be:

- clean

- accurate

- consistent with your public records

- fully functional

- and completely free of contradictions

If your address is different on the website than on your application? That **_will result in_** a rejection. If your corporate name is spelled differently? That **_will be_** a rejection. If half the pages are "Under Construction"? That **_will result in_** a rejection.

A lender wants to see a business that has taken the time to establish a professional presence. A website is proof of existence in the modern world.

Without it, the bank assumes you are either unprepared or hiding something. Neither one helps your chances.

Mistake #8: No Business Experian® Score or No Dun & Bradstreet® Listing

Before you apply for a loan or a line of credit, you must have at least one business credit file in motion. Not perfect, not extensive, it just needs to be active.

This is where **Experian Business®** and **Dun & Bradstreet®** enter the picture.

Here is what most applicants get wrong:

They think business credit will magically appear the moment they incorporate. It doesn't.

They think their personal credit will carry their business credit. It won't.

They think the lender will give them credit first, and then they'll build history later.

That's not how the system works.

Business credit must already exist, even in a small, early-stage form, before most lenders will take a company seriously.

A business **Experian®** file and **Dun & Bradstreet (D&B)®** file prove:

- The business is real.

- The business is active.

- The business pays bills.

- The business has suppliers.

- The business has a track record. (Even a short one helps.)

The fastest way to build early business credit is simple:

1. Order supplies from vendors that report.

2. Pay early, not just on time.

3. Keep everything consistent: name, address, phone number.

4. Avoid anything that looks forced, manipulated, or manufactured.

And here is a warning:

Do NOT buy trade lines or "credit boosting" packages. Lenders know how to spot them. **D&B®** knows how to spot them. **Experian®** knows how to spot them. Once flagged, you will have an uphill battle getting unflagged.

One legitimate shortcut, and it's the only shortcut I endorse, is purchasing **D&B's CreditBuilder Program®**.

It's expensive but worth it because it:

- allows you to check your **D&B PayDex Score®**

- lets you add your real vendor accounts

- ensures your file is complete

- verifies your information with **D&B®** directly

When your business credit file is clean, consistent, and active, lenders take you seriously. When it's missing or messy, lenders assume you're not ready, and they decline you without any hesitation.

Mistake #9: Not Having a Credit-Qualified Officer Sitting on Your Board of Directors

Of all the mistakes business owners make, this one sits comfortably in the top three. Banks may act as if they care about your business plan, your mission statement, your dreams, and your exciting new idea, but the truth is simple: **They care about who is steering the ship.** If the captain has bad credit, too much debt, late payments, or a thin personal credit file, the lender sees one thing: risk.

Banks learned long ago that a company is only as trustworthy as the financially responsible adult in the room. This is why they want at least one person on your board of directors who can demonstrate solid personal financial responsibility. When I say solid, I'm not talking about *"I pay my bills most of the time."* I'm talking about a **mid-700 FICO® score**, low credit card utilization (**30 percent** or less), a multi-year credit history, and a clean track record with past lenders.

Without someone like this listed as a board member, the bank underwriter won't waste time digging into your business. They'll stamp your application *"DECLINED"* and toss it into the pile where dreams go to die.

Now in many cases, business owners assume they can simply put themselves down as the credit-qualified officer. But what if your own credit took a beating during COVID? What if you've had a rough patch, medical bills, a divorce, or a bankruptcy? What if your credit is fine but not strong enough to impress a bank asking for a personal guarantor? This is where many business owners stumble: **They submit the application anyway**, hoping the bank won't look too closely. Trust me, they will. The bank's underwriting system evaluates the board members before it ever touches the business. If they see weak credit, the computer system kicks the application out before a human ever sees it.

However, you do have options …

You can ask a trusted business associate, a financially responsible sibling, a close friend, or even a parent to serve on your board as an officer. They won't be responsible for running your business or showing up for board meetings. They simply serve as financial credibility. Many people are happy to help once they understand the structure and the protections in place. But, and this is a very big "but," you must be honest with them.

If something goes sideways, if you miss a payment, or if your business spirals out of control because you didn't manage your cash flow, **their personal credit is on the hook.** The bank will call them before they call you. The bank will expect them to make the late payment. And if they don't? Their **FICO®** score gets clobbered.

I've seen friendships end over this. I've seen brothers stop speaking for years. I've seen family Thanksgiving dinner invitations canceled. You do not want to be the reason your mother, your newly nominated CFO-candidate, now refuses to let you through her front door because she just got a delinquency notice alert from Chase Bank® regarding your new business.

If you don't want to risk damaging a personal relationship, there is another option: **Hire a professional CFO to sit on your board of directors.** Yes, it costs money. No, it isn't cheap. But if the candidate has strong credit, a deep financial resume, and prior success securing business funding for corporations, they can dramatically improve your chances. The Wilshire Financial Group, for example, can assist you in finding the right CFO/Director candidates who will sit on your board for a pre-negotiated percentage and lend their creditworthiness to the corporation.

Their resumes alone can often influence banks to approve loans.

Just remember: Whether it's your mom, your aunt, your best friend, or a paid professional CFO, the principle remains the same: Banks want someone on the board who can demonstrate personal financial responsibility and pay their bills on time. In the bank loan officer's eye, this indicates the company will also manage its finances responsibly. More importantly, it meets the bank's underwriting computer program requirement.

Mistake #10: Moving Forward Without Answers—The Silent Killer of Business Funding

This final mistake is the one that quietly destroys more business loan applications than any other: **proceeding without knowing what you're doing. Aka** *"winging it."*

You would be surprised how many entrepreneurs submit loan applications with unanswered questions floating around in their heads. They don't know how to structure their paperwork. Don't know which officer should be listed where. They don't understand which credit file the bank is going to pull. They don't know their own Experian Business profile is outdated. They don't understand the bank underwriting process. They don't know the difference between a hard credit pull and a soft credit pull. They don't confirm their corporate status with the Secretary of State. They don't confirm that their address is showing correctly with 411. They don't even check whether their website has a functioning *"Contact Us"* page.

And then they wonder why the bank denied them.

Let me make this perfectly clear: **When you don't know the answer to a question that can affect your loan approval and potentially squash your dream of getting the money you need to start your own business, or perhaps the money you need to**

save or expand your existing business … you should not guess, hope, or assume. You should call an expert. You've got one chance, and you must get this right …

I would like to share a quick story with you.

My last year in high school, I was offered a night employment position with a Newhouse/Hearst Corporation-owned newspaper. It was a good-paying union job, I was 18 years old, there were pretty girls working there, it sounded interesting, what did I know? I worked there for exactly four years. After completing a four-year apprenticeship program with the International Typographical Union, I was officially a Journeyman Printer. At that time in history, newspapers around the world were entering the "new computer age," and they began to evolve from hot-metal lead typesetting machines and printing presses to computer digital typesetting. Thousands of printers were being laid off. Interestingly, so much for the thousands of dollars we paid weekly in ITU union dues … The union was powerless. And, I had just become the low man on the journeyman totem pole. The very same day I became a journeyman printer … I was laid off from my job at the newspaper.

That did it for me!

I decided then and there I didn't like working for other people. Allowing someone else to hold control over my financial future was not for me.

I went into business for myself.

It was a good decision. My first year in business …

I made my first million dollars. The year was 1975, and I was 23 years old. A million dollars in 1975 had the same buying power as roughly **$6 million to $6.02 million dollars today (early 2026),** depending on the inflation index, with the common Consumer Price Index (CPI) (go to https://www.bls.gov/cpi/) showing it's around **$6,024,572**, meaning prices have increased over six times since then, due to about 3.58 percent average annual inflation over the last 51 years.

To this day, I've never been employed at a job working for anyone again.

I have been self-employed now for over 50 years.

During that time, I've been rich, I've been short on cash, and everything in between, and I will tell you this with absolute confidence:

Being rich is better.

The only ordinary people, like you and me, who even have a snowball's chance in hell at earning $1,000,000.00+ a year, even in today's burgeoning economy, are self-employed entrepreneurs and business owners.

Entrepreneurs love to dive right in. They love to sprint into action. They believe that instincts are enough, and sometimes they are. However, instinct and action are only half of the equation. You're going to need some start-up cash and rainy-day cash, and now you know exactly how and where to get it … the banks!

John Dillinger was once asked, *"Why do you rob banks?"* His answer was, *"Because that's where the money is …"*

Major banks and business underwriters operate under strict federal guidelines. The smallest error—a mismatched address, an unlisted phone number, an improperly filed corporate document, a missing board member, an outdated Dun & Bradstreet® profile— can trigger an automatic denial and, in some instances, a six-month "financial stress alert" that follows your corporation from bank to bank like a black cloud.

This is why expert help exists.

If you do not have a corporation that is old enough or compliant enough to qualify for funding, call someone who specializes in fixing exactly that. The Wilshire Financial Group Inc.®, for example, engineers companies, aged and bank-seasoned corporations specifically designed to pass all current underwriting criteria. They have an in-house staff of experts, bookkeepers, a payroll agent, an IRS Enrolled Agent, tax preparers, a notary, loan specialists, and even operators who have been trained to answer business calls professionally, so the banks hear the background sound of business instead of a barking dog or crying baby.

With the right knowledge and guidance, you can avoid every mistake on this list.

Proceeding with the wrong assumptions, you can sabotage your own success without even realizing it.

You now know the 10 biggest mistakes business owners make when applying for credit. These are the errors that quietly sink applications every single day. Learn them. Memorize them. Internalize them until they feel like second nature. When you avoid these mistakes and follow the step-by-step loan application principles outlined in this book, you will make the shift from stage three, conscious competence, to stage four: **unconscious competence**, where knowing how to obtain business funding becomes almost automatic.

And once you reach that point, everything changes.

Chapter 9

Building Credit with the Business Credit Reporting Bureaus

"Never give up on a dream just because of the time it will take to accomplish it. The time will pass anyway."

—Earl Nightingale

Every business owner eventually reaches the point where they realize that personal hustle may not be enough. Cash flow matters, profitability matters, but access to credit is what turns a small business operation into something that can grow without choking itself or being stopped in its tracks by unexpected road blocks. That's where the business credit reporting bureaus come in.

They sit quietly in the background, collecting data, creating profiles, and influencing how lenders view your company long before you ever shake anyone's hand at a bank. You can choose to ignore them, or you can learn how they work and make them work in your favor. This chapter is about exactly that: understanding the landscape and making smart moves inside it.

Now, if you want to build real business credit, your first job is to get your profile started the correct way. The first step begins with applying for your **D&B Number®**. Think of it as your business's official ID in their system. Without it, you don't exist to them. Lenders can't look you up. Vendors can't report your payment history. And nobody extending you credit can pull a profile on you. Entrepreneurs sometimes assume their EIN is enough; it isn't. The **D&B® Number** is its own identifier, and you want it in place as early in your business journey as possible.

Once you apply for that number, you're not finished. You've opened the door, but you still need to make sure the data sitting on the other side is correct. That means verifying your basic business information: the legal name, the physical business address, your EIN, the phone number that's listed *and* answered during business hours, and any additional details they ask for. Accuracy matters. You can do everything else right and still run into problems if the bureau can't match your company to the correct records. This is one of the reasons people get denied for credit lines they should have qualified for: simple mismatches in basic information.

Once your profile is verified, you're ready for the part that most business owners skip over or misunderstand: your **D&B PayDex Score®**. Every lender doesn't speak the same language, but almost all of them pay attention to this one. The **PayDex® Score** runs from 0 to 100 and reflects how reliably your business pays the people it does business with, vendors, suppliers, net-30 accounts, and similar credit relationships. A score of 100 means your payments are flawless. A score of 0 means you're either paying late, paying inconsistently, or not paying at all. And everything in between tells some story about how you operate.

Here is the important part: This score isn't just about paying on time. It's about paying **early**. In my world, and in the world of lenders, "on time" is the bare minimum. If you want the strongest score possible, pay your vendor invoices **the day you receive them**. That earns you what the bureau calls an ***"anticipate rating,"*** the highest tier they award. It's also the easiest way to signal that your business is healthy, disciplined, liquid, and trustworthy. Every future lender looking at your file will see that pattern and draw the correct conclusions about you.

As you use more vendors, place more orders, and keep paying early, your record grows thicker and more credible. That history becomes your business reputation on paper. Without it, you remain a question mark. With it, you gain leverage, lower interest rates, higher limits, and easier approvals.

While you're building that record, there is something else you need to be aware of: **monitoring your file**. You can pull your **D&B®** credit report once every 30 days without raising any flags. Check it more often than that, and their system may treat it as suspicious behavior. An alert gets attached to your file, and you don't want that. It doesn't hurt your score, but it tells lenders that something unusual is happening. So pace yourself and be smart about your checks.

If you're serious about building credit quickly, their **Credit Builder Plus®** program can speed things up. At the moment, it runs about $149 a month. Is it required? No, it is not. Is it helpful? Absolutely, it is. You get faster verification of vendor accounts, quicker updates to your profile, and 24-hour access to information. More importantly, their support team actually knows what they're doing, and getting corrections made through them is faster than trying to navigate the usual channels.

Before I conclude this subject, let me be perfectly clear: **You do not need vendor credit or a perfect PayDex® Score to get approved for large unsecured business lines.** But having the **D & B® Number** set up and having your business listed correctly is a smart step in your foundational setup. You're building a house. You want the walls straight and the floors level before you start loading everything in.

How the PayDex® Score Works and Why It Matters

Once your **D&B®** profile is set up and verified, you're officially in the system, but you still haven't built anything yet. The bureau isn't going to assign you a strong score just because you exist. You have to feed the system the correct information, and that happens through your payment activity with vendors and suppliers. This is where the **PayDex Score®** becomes the centerpiece of your business credit identity.

A lot of entrepreneurs misunderstand why this score matters so much. They assume lenders look only at bank activity, tax returns, revenue, and cash flow. Those things matter, but lenders don't want to waste time digging through your history if they can see a pattern of behavior somewhere else first. The **PayDex Score®** is that shortcut. It's a clean signal. It shows whether your business treats its obligations with discipline or with sloppiness. And believe me, lenders notice the difference.

As I mentioned earlier, the score runs from zero to 100. A perfect 100 tells lenders you make payments ahead of time and you maintain excellent financial habits. I have personally never seen a score of 100. But that's fine because a **PayDex®** score in the 80s is considered strong, industry-standard "on time, every time." Anything below that may start to raise questions. And when a lender sees a score in the 50s or 60s, they assume you're either struggling or ignoring your obligations. Neither is good for approvals.

D&B® receives this data from reporting vendors. If a vendor doesn't report, the bureau can't use it, which is why choosing your vendors wisely is part of the credit-building strategy. When vendors report, the bureau logs the number of payments, the size of those payments, and how early or late each one was. They use that pattern to calculate your monthly **PayDex Score®**. You don't get to send them receipts or narratives manually. The bureau trusts only verified data coming directly from the companies you owe money to. This keeps the system cleaner and prevents people from manipulating their profiles.

Now, let's talk about speed. You can build a good **PayDex Score®** faster than most people think. The key is to set up vendor accounts early, use them, and pay them immediately. Not "before the due date," not "within terms," not "just in time"—**immediately.** Think of it the same way you think of customer service. The businesses that stand out are the ones that go beyond what's required. Early payments work the same way. They generate the "anticipate" rating that the bureau likes to see. And once you hit that pattern consistently, your score stabilizes in the top bracket.

This is where discipline matters. Don't order more than you can handle. Don't overextend yourself. Use vendor credit strategically. If you need office supplies, buy a little. If you need printing, buy a little. The point isn't to create debt, it's to create payment history. A small invoice paid early does just as much for your score as a large invoice paid early. That's something a lot of entrepreneurs don't realize.

As your score grows, opportunities open. Higher limits. Fast approvals. Lower rates. And even outside lenders, banks, credit unions, and specialty credit lines use this data as part of their underwriting models. They're looking for consistency. They want to see that you respect credit terms even when you don't have to. That tells them you will treat their money responsibly, too.

Now, let's touch on monitoring again, because it is one of the easiest places to make an unnecessary mistake. You will see your score update each month. That is enough. Pulling your report more often may trigger a system alert at **D&B®**. It doesn't "hurt" you, but it does create a note on your file that says: "This business is pulling their report more than usual." No lender wants to see unnecessary activity like that. It signals impatience or anxiety. Stick to once every thirty days unless you're disputing something or updating information.

Speaking of disputes, mistakes happen. Vendor data sometimes reports late or inaccurately. Addresses get mismatched. Business names get shortened or misspelled. These issues aren't the end of the world, but correcting them quickly is important. If your business name is listed incorrectly, lenders can't match your documents to the bureau profile. If a vendor reports a late payment incorrectly, it can drag your score down unnecessarily. Staying on top of your report each month helps catch these things before they cause real damage.

This is also where the **D&B Credit Builder Plus Program®** earns its keep. When you're inside their system at that level, you get faster access to corrections and updates. You're not stuck waiting on automated responses or long queues. You're dealing with real humans who can make adjustments and verify accounts more efficiently. For a business that wants to scale quickly, that speed can make a big difference.

Before we shift into the application side of all this, there is something I want to make absolutely clear. There are business owners who think they must have a perfect **PayDex Score®** before applying for major funding. That is simply not true. Solid unsecured business lines, bank loans, and high-limit programs do not require vendor credit. They do not require a high **D&B PayDex Score®**. You could have a brand-new **D&B®** number and still get approved if your business is structured correctly and you follow the steps outlined in this book.

Still, having a strong foundation never hurts. Being listed with **D&B®** creates credibility. It puts you on the radar. And as your company grows, the benefits compound. You save money, you increase access, and you make yourself easier to approve for the things you will want later, whether that's vehicle financing, equipment leasing, or long-term commercial lending.

This is the part of business credit that's rarely explained properly. Everyone talks about "build your vendor credit," but they miss why it matters and how to do it without wasting time or money. Your goal isn't to become a "trade line collector." Your goal is to build a *trustworthy* business identity that lenders will respect.

Building and Maintaining a Strong Business Credit Profile

Once you understand how the **PayDex Score®** works, the next step is putting the right habits in place. Building business credit is not complicated, but it does require consistency. Most owners struggle not because the process is difficult, but because they either skip steps or try to rush things. Credit bureaus don't respond to shortcuts. They respond to patterns. Establish the right patterns, and the system takes care of the rest.

Start with your vendor accounts. This is the part where you build the actual history that **D&B®** records every month. Apply for credit with companies that you're already using in your business: office supplies, ink, printing, janitorial services, packaging, or whatever industry-specific materials you need. The key is to select vendors that report to **D&B®**. Not every company does. Some provide net-30 terms but don't send any data to the bureaus. That's fine for your cash flow, but it does nothing for your **Dun & Bradstreet PayDex Score®**. You want vendors that extend credit *and* report your payment activity. That's the combination that creates measurable score improvement.

After opening those accounts, place small, manageable orders. Your goal isn't to run up balances. Your goal is to show consistent activity. You don't need large purchases. You just need regular ones, something you can pay off immediately without thinking twice. When the invoice comes in, pay it right away. If you want the highest rating in their system, don't wait for the due date. Pay the invoice the day it hits your inbox. That habit is what builds the top-tier "anticipate" rating most entrepreneurs never reach.

At the same time, keep an eye on your credit utilization ratio. This concept tends to confuse people because they associate it with personal credit scoring. While business credit works differently, the idea is similar: Lenders want to see that you're not pushing your credit to the limit. If you have a $10,000 vendor line, don't sit at $8,000 every month. Keep usage below 30 percent. That sends a message that you're running your operation responsibly, not scrambling to float expenses.

Another key piece is relationships. Entrepreneurs love to talk about automation, but when it comes to business credit, old-fashioned communication still matters. Your vendors and suppliers are not just billing departments; they're quiet partners in your credit-building journey. Staying responsive, paying early, and communicating clearly when you place orders or need adjustments goes a long way. When people know you're reliable, they're more likely to extend additional terms, increase limits, and process reports quickly. Those small things make a noticeable difference over the long run.

Now, let's talk about maintenance. Once your profile starts to grow, you need to treat it like any other business asset. Review your **Dun & Bradstreet PayDex Score®** regularly, ideally once every month. Don't overdo it. Pulling your report too often triggers those irritating flags we talked about earlier, and you don't want anything in your file that raises unnecessary questions. Once a month is enough. Check your business name, address, phone number, and officer information. If anything is incorrect or incomplete, fix it right away.

Errors are more common than most people think. A vendor may report something late. A payment may appear as overdue even though you paid early. The system may merge or shorten your business name incorrectly. These problems don't mean your business is in trouble; it's just the nature of large reporting systems. But they need to be corrected because even small inaccuracies can affect how lenders see you. If you're part of the **D&B Credit Builder Plus**

Program®, this process becomes much simpler. Their team can update your information faster, verify vendor accounts sooner, and correct mistakes without long delays.

While we're on the subject of corrections, let me repeat something because it's important: If you notice an error, address it immediately. Don't wait. Don't assume it will fix itself. Bureau data only updates when someone takes action, and in business credit, especially when you're preparing for large financing, clean data matters.

Once your vendor history is stable and your **PayDex® Score** is consistently strong, you're in a much better position to apply for credit with companies outside your immediate vendor network. This is when retail business accounts, fleet cards, and even certain revolving lines become available. But be selective. Don't apply for every line you see. Choose accounts that make sense for your business and support your long-term structure. Every approval strengthens your credibility, and every well-maintained account builds the patterns lenders want to see.

Let's also clear up a misconception many entrepreneurs fall for: You do not need dozens of trade lines to build a strong profile. A handful of well-managed accounts does far more for you than 20 neglected ones. Five to seven strong, activity-driven vendor lines are more than enough to build the early foundation. Focus on quality, not quantity.

This is also the stage where many business owners start thinking ahead to bank credit cards, unsecured lines, and full business loans. The vendor history your business is building now makes those easier later. Even though banks don't rely solely on vendor data, they look at the whole picture. When they see clean reporting, early payments, low utilization, and a disciplined pattern, they feel more confident offering higher limits and better terms.

Credit building is not about racing to a finish line. It's about proving consistency. The same discipline that positions you for strong funding opportunities also protects your business in the long run. You're not just trying to get approved, you're building a lending profile that works for you year after year.

The final piece in this section is simple: **Your goal is a PayDex® score of 80 or above.**

Treat your business credit like an asset that grows with attention. The routines you set today, the early payments, the accurate information, and the steady usage, will carry your company as it scales. Once these habits are in place, maintaining a strong credit profile becomes second nature.

Business Experian®, What They Track, and How It Affects You

By the time you've built a solid foundation with **D& B®,** you've already put yourself ahead of most business owners. But there is another player in the business credit world, one that carries a different kind of weight.

Experian Business Credit Reporting®

Now, let me be direct with you. You don't have to hunt these people down. They will find you. Every business eventually shows up in their system because they pull from sources that don't require your permission. Banks, lenders, credit unions, and financial institutions feed them data automatically. The moment your business receives or uses any form of cash-based credit, business credit cards, loans, or lines of credit, **Experian ®** reporting jumps into the picture. And unlike **D&B®,** which mainly focuses on your payment history with vendors and suppliers, the **Experian Business Credit®** bureau deals with the deep end of the pool: financial credit used for cash.

What they track is simple to understand but incredibly important. They monitor the accounts that involve money actually being lent to your business: credit cards, charge cards, business term loans, unsecured lines, secured lines, and other forms of financial credit. Anything tied to real dollars borrowed and repaid ends up in their database. This makes them the most serious bank bureaus. When a lender wants to understand how you behave with actual borrowed money, not trade lines, not vendor accounts, but real banking relationships, they look at Experian® reporting.

One critical difference is the kind of scoring model they use. While **Dun & Bradstreet®** focuses heavily on promptness with vendor terms, **Experian®** reporting evaluates risk from a bank lender's perspective. They look at how much credit you've been extended, how much of it you use, whether you pay on time, whether you revolve balances, and whether you've ever been late or overextended. In other words, they measure how you handle real cash obligations. Even your bank credit cards get tracked here. If you're irresponsible with a business credit card, maxing it out, making minimum payments, letting balances linger, this bureau will show it.

The good news? You don't have to "build" anything here. You don't need to submit forms, apply for numbers, or chase down activation steps. Once your business starts moving real financial credit, the reporting happens automatically. Your job is to make sure the information that shows up is correct. Start by checking your business name, address, and officer information. It should match your corporate documents exactly. If the bureau reports your business under an incorrect variation of your name, a bank reviewing your application may not be able to match records. That simple mismatch is enough to cause confusion or even denials.

Because **Experian®** gathers data automatically, errors can occur. A bank may send information to an old address. A credit card provider might shorten your LLC name in a way the system misinterprets. A lender might report usage without updating your new credit limit. These aren't disasters, but they can create unnecessary problems. That's why you review your Experian® profile periodically, just enough to stay ahead of mistakes, not obsessively. Like with **D&B®**, moderation matters. Don't pound their system with constant pulls. Lenders don't like seeing erratic behavior.

Here is something important to understand: Banks trust Experian® because the data comes directly from them. There is no middleman vendor reporting manually. There is no lag from a printing company waiting to close out invoices. It's real financial information, reported by institutions that are heavily regulated. For that reason, this bureau rarely makes adjustments based solely on your claim. If something is wrong, you typically need supporting documentation from the reporting lender. When you do things correctly, this is not a problem. When you are sloppy with your paperwork or slow in updating your business documents, it becomes a headache.

Now let's talk strategy. You don't "game" **Experian Business Credit Reporting®.** You respect it. The system rewards discipline. Pay your business credit cards on time. Keep utilization reasonable. Don't let high revolving balances become your normal operating method. Lenders can see patterns. If you're constantly sitting at 90 percent utilization, lenders interpret that as instability. If you stay below 30 percent and pay early when possible, lenders see reliability. Just like personal credit, business credit thrives on consistency.

Experian® also gives lenders something **Dun & Bradstreet®** can't, a picture of how your business handles cash under pressure. Vendor lines don't show whether you can manage revolving accounts. Net-30 terms don't reveal how you handle larger financing. **Experian®** reflects real borrowing behavior, and lenders weigh it accordingly.

Here is where the two systems work together. **Dun & Bradstreet®** helps you establish early discipline and a strong identity as a responsible business. **Experian®** confirms how you behave once you start handling real financial bank credit. When both bureaus show clean, stable, accurate information, lenders have very few reasons to hesitate. You become the kind of borrower banks prefer: predictable, responsible, and easy to underwrite.

One last thing before we close the chapter. Many entrepreneurs worry about "doing everything perfectly" before applying for serious funding. You don't have to do everything perfectly. If you follow the steps in this book, structure your business correctly, set up your identity properly, avoid red flags, and choose the right lenders, you will be approved. **Dun & Bradstreet®** helps. **Experian Business Credit Reporting®** matters to the banks. But neither one replaces the fundamental structure you've put in place. They support it. They strengthen it. They validate your discipline.

Lenders aren't looking for perfection. They're looking for reliability. The habits you're establishing with your vendors and the discipline you maintain with your financial credit become your business credit reputation. That reputation grows with you. Treat it like an asset, and it will open doors that stay open.

Chapter 10

Managing Your Business Credit Profile

"I haven't reported my missing credit card to the police because whoever stole it is spending much less than my wife."

—Ilie Nastase

Most business owners learn early that borrowing money is easy. Managing credit is where discipline shows up. Anyone can open a card, take on a loan, or get approved for vendor terms. The real work starts when those accounts begin reporting. Your corporate credit profile becomes a living, breathing reflection of how you run your business, not the way you *talk* about running it, not the way you *plan* to run it, but the way you actually operate day to day. Lenders look at that profile long before they look at your face. Suppliers use it to decide what terms to extend. Even potential partners may use it to gauge whether you're steady, reliable, and worth doing business with.

This chapter is about taking ownership of that profile. Not reacting after something goes wrong, not scrambling to fix damage after a denial, but managing it intentionally so it becomes a strength you can lean on. When you understand how business credit works, you stop guessing. You stop hoping. You start building a predictable financial environment for your company, one that helps you negotiate, expand, and operate confidently.

A strong credit profile doesn't happen by accident. It's built through consistent habits: monitoring, correcting, protecting, and maintaining. Some owners make the mistake of thinking their business credit runs itself. It doesn't. A credit bureau only knows what gets reported. If a vendor files something incorrectly, if a bank updates an address wrong, if an account you closed years ago shows as active, the bureau doesn't chase you down to fix it. You have to be the one paying attention.

Your corporate credit profile contains several key elements: payment history, credit utilization, age of accounts, public filings, and even the number of applications you've made. All of these form the picture lenders see when they're deciding whether to trust you with their money. That's why managing your profile isn't just about getting a good score; it's about building the type of reputation that keeps doors open. A clean, consistent credit profile makes negotiating with suppliers easier. It helps you secure better terms and better rates. It removes friction in areas you don't even realize are affected by credit.

Before going deeper, it's important to make a distinction many people miss: **Your corporate credit and your personal credit are separate, but they influence each other more than most people think.**

You can run a strong business, but if you let your personal credit get sloppy, the problems will follow you. And if your business credit profile is poorly managed, lenders may default back to your personal credit, putting your personal finances at risk. The goal of this book, and this chapter in particular, is to keep both credit files clean, separate, and strong.

Managing a business credit profile starts with one simple idea: awareness. You cannot fix what you don't see. You cannot protect yourself from fraud you're not watching for. You cannot dispute errors you never notice. That's why monitoring your credit profile is one of the first and most important habits to build. You're not checking out of paranoia; you're checking because the credit system is not perfect. Data gets misreported all the time. Accounts show up that shouldn't. Payment histories get misaligned. And yes, fraud does happen. You want to catch those problems when they're small, not after they've ballooned into a denial or a liability.

Fraud isn't the only threat. Basic administrative errors cause just as many issues. A misspelled business name. An outdated business address. A phone number that no longer matches the one listed on your website. These things sound minor, but lenders take consistency seriously. When they see mismatched records, they don't assume "simple mistake." They assume risk. The more inconsistencies in your profile, the more likely your application is to get slowed down or denied altogether.

Another part of managing your business credit profile is knowing where your data comes from. Most business owners can list their lenders but have no idea which bureaus those lenders report to, how often they report, or even what format the data takes. Vendor accounts behave differently from bank accounts. Banks report differently from leasing companies. And each bureau organizes that data in its own way. When you know how those systems work, you can build your profile deliberately instead of accidentally.

Now let's talk about something many business owners overlook: Healthy credit management is proactive, not reactive.

Waiting until you need financing to start cleaning up your credit is like waiting until the day of the exam to learn the material. It can be done, but it's stressful and avoidable. The time to monitor your reports is when things are calm. The time to correct errors is before you apply. The time to build a positive history is before you walk into negotiations.

A strong corporate credit profile also requires smart behavior with your accounts. Paying vendors early, keeping utilization low, spacing out applications, and maintaining open communication with suppliers: All of these habits shape how your business is perceived. Managing credit isn't glamorous work. You're not going to brag about it at a networking event. But it is one of the most powerful long-term tools you have for building financial stability.

And that brings us to the real purpose of this chapter. I'm not here to scare you or bury you in technicalities. I'm here to give you a clear roadmap for managing your business credit intelligently. We're going to cover how to monitor your credit reports, how to detect and fix errors, how to protect yourself from fraud, and how to build strong working relationships with lenders and suppliers.

By the time you finish this chapter, you will know how to keep your credit profile clean, accurate, and strong, not just for the next loan you apply for, but for the life of your business.

Protecting Your Business Credit: Fraud, Errors, and Staying Ahead of Trouble

Business owners often assume credit problems come from careless spending or poor decision-making. Sometimes that's true. More often, the problems show up because the owner wasn't paying attention. Errors slip in quietly. Fraud creeps in slowly. A small issue sits unaddressed for too long and becomes something bigger than it ever needed to be. Managing your business credit isn't about fear; it's about being responsible enough to protect what you've built.

Your corporate credit is an extension of your business identity. If that identity gets compromised, through fraud, sloppy reporting, or simple misunderstandings, it affects everything connected to it. Financing, partnerships, supplier terms, and even insurance rates can be influenced by the health and accuracy of your credit profile. That's why protecting both your personal and business credit isn't optional. It's a core part of running a stable company.

Let's start with fraud, because it's far more common than most people realize. Corporate identity theft is one of the fastest-growing forms of fraud. You don't have to lose your wallet or misplace a document for it to happen. Sometimes, a criminal only needs your business name, an EIN, and a mail drop to start opening accounts. Other times, someone tries to piggyback on your business's clean profile to run up charges under your name. Fraud doesn't always look like "someone drained a bank account." Sometimes it shows up on your credit report as a mystery account, a strange inquiry, or a credit line you never requested.

That's why monitoring your credit profile is the first line of defense. By reviewing your business reports regularly, you spot the things that don't belong, the accounts you didn't open, the addresses you've never used, and the sudden inquiries that don't align with your recent activity. When you catch these issues early, you can shut them down before they damage your creditworthiness or your financial standing.

Errors can be just as damaging as fraud. A simple mistake by a vendor, bank, or reporting agency can quietly drag down your credit for months without you noticing. Maybe a vendor reports a payment late because their system updates slowly. Maybe a bank forgets to update an account as closed. Maybe your business name was shortened or spelled incorrectly when the lender sent data to the bureau. These are mundane problems, but they create real consequences: lower scores, declined applications, higher interest rates, and tighter credit terms.

The bureaus don't correct errors automatically because they don't know something's wrong unless someone tells them. That someone is you. When you see inaccurate information, you dispute it. You contact the vendor or lender and request updated reporting. You provide documentation. You follow through until the data is corrected. This isn't exciting work, but it is essential. Clean information equals trust. And business credit is built on trust, even more than it's built on money.

Protecting your corporate credit goes deeper than reviewing reports. You also need to safeguard your business information. Criminals don't always need inside access; they often rely on publicly available details. Keep your EIN secure. Limit who handles sensitive business data. Use strong password protection on any system connected to banking or financial records. Be careful about email scams and fraudulent requests for account updates. A single sloppy moment can expose your company to a long list of headaches.

And let's not ignore the personal side. Many business owners treat their personal credit as if it exists on a separate planet. It doesn't. If your personal identity gets compromised, your Social Security number is stolen, or your personal accounts are breached, those problems can bleed into your business credit. Fraudsters aren't sophisticated criminals most of the time. They're opportunists. If they get through one door, they try the next one. Protecting your personal credit is part of protecting your business credit. The two are connected through you.

Once you're monitoring your profile regularly, you will start to recognize patterns. You will know what "normal" looks like, so you can catch what isn't. And when something doesn't look right, you act. You don't wait for the next billing cycle. You don't wait for a lender to contact you. You take control immediately. That's what responsible credit management looks like.

Here is another part most people overlook: **Fraud rarely starts big. It starts small.** A small test charge or a simple inquiry. A low-limit account. It's almost like someone tapping your window to see if the glass is loose. That's why early detection matters. By spotting the problem at the first sign, you avoid the damage entirely.

Credit monitoring services can help, but choose wisely. Some services bombard you with alerts that mean nothing. Others provide meaningful updates when something changes on your report: new accounts, credit pulls, balance shifts, address updates, and so on. Whether you use free reports or a paid service, consistency is the goal. You want a rhythm. You want to check your corporate credit proactively, not reactively.

Monitoring is only half the job. Acting on what you find is the other half. When you spot something incorrect, you dispute it. When you recognize suspicious activity, you report it. When a vendor misreports a payment, you request a correction. And if the situation warrants it, you place a fraud alert or freeze your credit profile to prevent further damage. You're not being paranoid, you're protecting your business.

By building the habit of watching your credit, you strengthen your financial foundation. You catch issues early, you correct them quickly, and you prevent minor problems from turning into setbacks. And once you get in the habit, managing your credit becomes less of a chore and more of a natural part of running your business.

That is the mindset we're building as we move deeper into this chapter. Credit protection isn't about waiting for trouble; it's about staying ahead of it.

Monitoring Your Credit Reports the Right Way (Without Creating Problems)

Most people think "monitor your credit" means glancing at a report once in a while. In business, that's not monitoring, that's just wishful thinking. Real monitoring is a habit. It's a system. And it's one of the most important responsibilities you have as a business owner. Your credit reports tell the story of your company's financial behavior. They show lenders how consistent you are, how risky you are, and how seriously you take your obligations. If you want that story to be accurate, you have to watch it.

Monitoring your business credit isn't busywork. It's preventive maintenance. The same way you check the oil in a car before the engine starts smoking, you check your credit reports before the problems cost you money or opportunities. You're doing this to protect yourself, not because it's fun, and not because the bureaus do a perfect job tracking your information. They don't. They're massive systems with hundreds of data sources feeding in constantly.

Mistakes are common. The owners who succeed are the ones who pay attention.

Let's break down why monitoring matters so much.

First, you're checking for errors.

This is the most obvious reason, yet it's the one that business owners overlook the most. Errors can show up in any part of your report. A payment misreported by a vendor. A balance is listed incorrectly. An account is displayed as open even though you closed it. An address is left over from years ago. A business name is wrong. These details seem small, but they affect your profile. Think of it from a lender's perspective: If the information doesn't match the application, they see uncertainty, not a "simple typo."

And lenders do not like uncertainty.

Second, you're watching for fraud.

Fraud in the business world doesn't always look like dramatic theft. Sometimes it's a new credit inquiry you didn't make. Sometimes it's an account opened in your business name at a bank you've never spoken to. Sometimes it's a vendor account with a balance you don't recognize. Fraud starts small because criminals are testing you. They want to see whether anyone is watching. If you don't catch it early, you find out later when you're dealing with declined applications, damaged scores, or financial liability you didn't create.

Third, you're making sure your credit profile reflects your real, current business.

Businesses change. Addresses change. Ownership changes. Phone numbers change. If your profile doesn't keep up with those changes, lenders can't match your identity to your documents. And when there is a mismatch, lenders don't hunt down the problem; they simply deny the application or delay your approval. Monitoring regularly avoids that.

Now, let's talk about how to monitor correctly.

Most business owners jump straight to expensive credit monitoring subscriptions. Those can help, but they're not required. In consumer credit, you can pull your free reports from the three major bureaus, **Equifax®, Experian®,** and **TransUnion®**, once per year. If you spread them out every four months, you're essentially watching your credit year-round at zero cost. That's smart for your personal profile, and remember, your personal credit does matter in business lending more often than lenders admit.

On the business side, you will check your **D & B®** report no more than once every 30 days. Anything more than that potentially gets you flagged, and flagged accounts make lenders uncomfortable. When they see an alert on your file, they start asking questions, and the last thing you need is unnecessary attention during underwriting. So pace yourself. Once a month is enough to stay informed without raising any red flags.

Credit monitoring services can provide real-time alerts, which are helpful when you have a growing business with multiple accounts reporting activity. The key is choosing a service that provides meaningful updates, not endless notifications that don't matter. A good service alerts you when:

- a new account appears
- a lender updates a balance
- an inquiry hits your report
- your business profile information changes

- your score shifts unexpectedly
- a new address or phone number is attached to your file

Those alerts matter. They help you react quickly when something needs your attention.

Monitoring is only helpful if you're willing to act. When you see an error, you dispute it. When you find outdated information, you correct it. When a lender reports something incorrectly, you reach out and request a fix. Don't assume anything will "clear up on its own." Credit reports don't fix themselves. They stay as-is until someone pushes the correction through.

If you find evidence of fraud, unauthorized accounts, unknown inquiries, or changes you didn't make, you take immediate action. That means contacting the creditor, notifying the bureau, and placing a fraud alert or even a freeze if necessary. You're protecting your business identity, and your fast response matters.

Here is something I want you to keep in mind:
Monitoring is not a one-time event. It's a business routine.

The same way you check your financials, manage payroll, or track inventory, you monitor your credit. It's part of your operational rhythm. Successful companies aren't "lucky." They're consistent. And credit monitoring is one of the most consistent habits you can build to protect your financial future.

Monitoring also helps you understand your own business better. When you see how your usage affects your scores, how quickly payments are reported, and how different lenders behave, you become smarter in your financial decisions. You stop guessing. You start anticipating. You can see which behaviors strengthen your profile, and which ones weaken it.

Without monitoring, you're flying blind. With monitoring, you're in control.

You want to be the kind of business owner who knows what's happening inside your credit file, not the one who finds out there is a problem after the fact. The best time to fix an issue is when it's small. The second-best time is right now. The worst time is when a lender rejects your application, and you're scrambling to understand why.

Regular monitoring prevents that. It keeps your file clean, accurate, and ready for any financing opportunity that comes your way.

The Truth About Trade Lines and Authorized Users, and Why Shortcuts Can Sometimes Backfire

There is a part of credit management that most people hear about long before they understand it: **buying trade lines** or becoming an **authorized user** on someone else's account. It's an attractive idea because it sounds fast. Add a strong trade line, get a quick boost, and watch your credit score jump. Simple, right? Except it's not simple. And in business credit, shortcuts can often do more harm than good.

Let's be clear about what these trade lines actually are. A trade line is simply an account on a credit report, a record of someone else's credit behavior. When you "buy" a trade line, you're paying someone else to place you as an authorized user on their credit account. Their history, age of their account, credit limit, and payment pattern get added to your report. If the account is clean and well-established, with a high limit, it can temporarily make your profile look stronger. That's why people chase these things.

But here is the part no one thinks about: You don't control that account. The donor does.

You're tying your financial reputation to someone else's behavior. If they're perfect, you benefit. If they slip even once, you take the hit. And you take it hard.

Imagine spending money to be added to someone's trade line, their perfect history lifts your score, and then one month in the future, just one, they miss a payment. Their mistake becomes your problem. Your score drops like a one-egg pudding. The lenders see the late mark. And there is nothing you can do about it because you were never the one making the payments in the first place. That's the hidden risk people overlook because they're focused only on a "quick credit score boost."

There is another danger: the integrity of the trade line seller.

This industry attracts some of the worst characters, fraudsters, manipulators, and people who know how desperate borrowers can get. Many of these sellers inflate results, hide the risks, or simply take your money and disappear. Even the ones who operate "legitimately" can't protect you from the possibility that the donor is only human and one day may slip up or close the account. It's your decision to make, but give it serious consideration before proceeding. Are you really willing to gamble your business credit profile on someone else's reliability?

And be advised that the credit bureaus are not blind to this behavior. Scoring models have evolved. The newer **FICO®** algorithms (especially **FICO 10T®**) are designed to identify and discount artificially added trade lines. Translation: the boost you think you're getting might not count the way you think. In some cases, it won't count at all. The bureaus know when something looks unnatural. They've been battling this behavior for years because it manipulates the system.

Let's say you get lucky. You add a trade line. It works. Your score jumps. You think you've found the magic formula. Does that guarantee approvals from banks? Not at all. Lenders don't approve solely on the score. They may look at income, cash flow, account history, business structure, inquiries, debt-to-credit ratios, and overall financial behavior. A single borrowed trade line isn't enough to override the bigger picture. At best, it helps slightly. At worst, it raises eyebrows.

You also have to consider cost. These trade line sellers don't work for free. They charge hundreds or even thousands of dollars for something temporary. The effect fades when the donor removes you, or when the bureaus filter it out, and then you're back where you started, except now you've spent money you could have used to build your business and real credit.

Let me say this clearly:

There is only one legitimate reason to ever consider taking the risk of adding a trade line to your credit profile ... reducing your debt-to-credit ratio (DTC).

And even then, the safest way to do it is through someone you personally know and trust. Not a stranger and certainly not a trade line broker. Someone who has a long, consistent history of responsible credit behavior and absolutely no reason to jeopardize their financial stability. Even then, it is only temporary support and certainly not a long-term strategy.

Here is the deeper truth: Shortcuts don't fix the underlying habits that caused the low credit score in the first place. If your credit is weak because of missed payments, high utilization, or constant applications, adding someone else's history doesn't solve any of that. You still need to develop the habits that build long-lasting creditworthiness: paying on time, keeping balances low, using credit responsibly, and maintaining a clean report.

This is why I rarely recommend trade lines to clients, and only when the relationship is personal, secure, and mutually understood. Even then, we use them carefully and only when the client needs temporary breathing room to correct their debt-to-credit ratios. I don't refer clients to outside trade line brokers. I don't trust the industry. Too many "scumbags, shit weasels, and bottom feeders," as I've said before, operate in that space. And when it comes to your financial future and identity, you don't gamble with it.

A strong credit profile comes from discipline, not shortcuts and tricks. Banks want to see consistent behavior, not borrowed credibility. They want to see consistent on-time payments. They want to see low utilization. They want to see smart decisions. They want to see stability and are looking for a long-term business relationship with you and your business.

If you invest your time into building your credit properly— monitoring your credit profiles, correcting errors, paying early, maintaining low balances, and managing relationships with vendors and lenders—you won't need shortcuts. You will have real credit. The kind no bureau can take away, no donor can ruin, and no scoring model can discount.

So here is the final takeaway from this chapter:

Your credit profile becomes an asset only when you build it with diligence and discipline. Shortcuts offer temporary boosts. Real credit offers long-term leverage. Choose the strategy that supports your business for years, not the one that just may disappear the moment someone other than yourself makes a mistake.

Chapter 11

Applying for Corporate Credit Cards and Loans

"I don't use a debit card. The safest thing is a credit card because you're using the bank's money. If someone accesses your information, they are stealing the bank's money, not yours."

—Frank Abagnale

Applying for business credit cards and loans sounds simple on paper. You fill out a form, hand over a few documents, and wait for a favorable decision. That's the surface-level version. In reality, lenders are studying you long before they approve anything. They're not looking for perfection; they're looking for predictability. They want to see whether your business behaves the way responsible borrowers behave, and whether you understand how credit works as a tool, not a lifeline.

This chapter is about more than checking a score and submitting applications. It's about preparing your business so every application you send out has the highest chance of approval and the lowest chance of creating unnecessary damage. When you understand what lenders actually look for, you approach the credit process from a position of strength, not hope.

Before you apply for anything, you start with a basic but essential step: **Checking Your Business Credit profile**.

Your **Experian®** business score is one of the most influential factors in most credit decisions. Many business owners apply blindly. They fire off applications without knowing how they look on paper. That's equivalent to walking into a bank interview without knowing whether or not you have spinach in your teeth. You should always check your business credit scores first. Then check your teeth.

Experian Business Credit® Reporting offers a free look at your business credit score, and there is no reason to skip it. The score you see tells you two things: how lenders see you today, and how prepared you are to apply. If your profile looks weak or contains errors, you fix the issues before you start submitting applications. What you do **before** applying matters just as much as what you list on the application itself.

Another major rule: **Limit yourself to one or, at most, two loan applications per month.**

Every application leaves a footprint. Too many inquiries clustered together make you look desperate or unstable, and lenders do not reward panic. A controlled, steady application pace helps you build credit without creating red flags. Remember, underwriting programs are written to be sensitive to patterns. They're programmed to approve borrowers who seldom apply for credit and loans, not applicants who are submitting multiple loan applications, trying to grab a credit line from every bank in town.

Once you've reviewed your business credit profiles, your next step is choosing the right business cards to apply for. Choosing the right card is not about chasing attractive bonuses. It's about finding cards that serve two purposes:

1. **They report to Business Experian® Reporting** (because you want the credit-building benefit).

2. **They support your business needs** (cash flow, business-oriented reward programs, low intro rates, APR, etc.).

Many business owners apply for any card they can find an application for. That is a rookie mistake. You want cards that contribute to your long-term financial profile, not cards that hand you a short-term reward.

Cards that report to **Experian® Business Credit Reporting** help build your financial credibility. They show how you behave with real money, not vendor terms. Lenders treat that data seriously. A good card used responsibly builds your business credit faster than trade accounts ever will.

The next part of the application process is often where business owners get tripped up: **documentation.**

Lenders will ask for very specific documents, your EIN, perhaps your **D&B®** number, articles of business formation, your current business license, banking resolution letter, and sometimes financial statements. These aren't optional. You cannot "wing it" or hope they'll ignore missing information. A clean, complete application is a signal to lenders that you know what you're doing.

A sloppy application makes you look unprepared. And unprepared borrowers don't get approvals.

Now let's talk about something lenders won't say out loud, but every experienced borrower knows:

Your attitude matters if you even get this far.

A banker wants to feel good about you. If they are asking for an interview, then they want to believe that you understand your own business, that you're confident, not arrogant, not panicked, not lost. **If you apply for "stated income" credit, the lender is asking for your optimistic income projections; be optimistic!**

They need to justify approving your loan application to their bosses. Show them you understand your numbers, your market, and your future plans. When you act as if you belong in the room, lenders respond positively.

If you walk in shaking, sweating through your shirt, dodging questions, or acting like you memorized your business plan the night before? You've already lost. Lenders aren't amused by uncertainty. They're not impressed by applicants who can't clearly explain what they need the money for. Confidence opens doors. Panic closes them.

Applying for business credit isn't a performance, but it is a communication test. Your job is to explain your business in a way that makes the lender say, "Approving this person makes sense."

Once you're ready to apply, choose only cards that match your credit score and business structure. *Banks publish minimum requirements for a reason.* Ignoring them is the fastest way to get an unnecessary denial. And every denial stays on your profile for six months. One denial is manageable. Multiple denials? They slow down the bus.

This section is meant to set the tone before we get into specific cards and lenders later in the chapter. Your success with business credit comes down to preparation, awareness, and presentation.

Don't chase business credit. Position yourself and your business so credit comes predictably, every time you apply.

By the time you finish this chapter, you will know exactly how to choose the right lenders, how to present your business properly, and how to avoid the common mistakes that sabotage most entrepreneurs before they ever get approved.

Preparing Your Business for Approval: Documents, Accuracy, and the Art of the Application

Before you apply for any business credit card or loan, you have to get your company's foundation in order. Most denials happen long before a lender ever looks at your score. They happen because something basic is missing, mismatched, or unclear. A lender doesn't want to chase you down for missing documents, or guess what your business actually does. They want clean, complete information. If you start with that, you're already ahead of most applicants.

Start with your documentation. You will need several items ready before applying, and it's better to gather them once and store them permanently in a dedicated "credit folder." That way, every time you apply, you're not scrambling.

Here are the basics you must have on hand before you saddle up and head to the bank:

- Your **EIN** letter from the IRS

- Your current **business license**

- Your **Articles of Incorporation** or **LLC formation documents**

- Your **banking resolution**

- Your **LLC Operating Agreement** or **Corporation Bylaws**

- Your State-issued Federal-issued **Photo ID**

- Sometimes basic **financial statements** (profit/loss statement, your balance sheet, or simple revenue summaries)

Banks may not ask for every item, but if you have them ready, the application process becomes smooth and predictable. Lenders appreciate applicants who are organized. Remember, they're not just evaluating your business; they are evaluating *you*. If you can't manage simple paperwork, potential lenders assume you can't manage borrowed money.

Once your documents are in order, the next step is accuracy. Your business identity must be consistent everywhere. That includes:

- Your corporate documents

- Your business bank account

- Your D & B® Profile

- Your Experian® Business Credit profile

- Your website address

- Your 441 listed business telephone listing

- Your completed loan application

If your business name appears slightly differently across systems, "ABC Technologies, LLC" in one place and "ABC Tech LLC" in another, banks don't assume they're the same company. They see a mismatch. Mismatches slow everything down. Some lenders will simply deny the application to avoid risk. And they won't call you to explain—they don't have the time.

Another mistake entrepreneurs make is underestimating how carefully lenders examine identity information. A lending officer isn't just checking your score; they're matching your documents line by line to make sure your business is structured, legitimate, and stable. Clean paperwork tells them you know what you're doing.

Now let's talk about filling out the application itself. This part is simple but often done poorly. Your job is to complete the form carefully, completely, and accurately. No blanks. No missing fields. No conflicting information. Any empty space may create doubt or a hold up on your loan approval.

And if you're applying for **stated income credit**, remember what *"stated income"* means. The lender is not asking you to predict the apocalypse or provide a 10-year Wall Street forecast. They're asking you to estimate your business activity in a way that shows confidence and competence. You're presenting a picture of your business that justifies the approval. Remember what I said earlier: be optimistic!

If you talk like you're unsure, the lender becomes unsure. If you downplay your potential, the lender may assume you don't have faith in your own business. If you act arrogant and come across like you're doing them a favor by applying, you might get the favor of a polite decline.

A bank wants to feel confident about approving your company. Your attitude either supports that or undermines it.

This brings us to presentation, an underrated part of getting approved. When you meet with a banker or have a phone interview, assume they're evaluating more than your answers. They're watching your confidence, your clarity, and your ability to communicate. If you're sweating bullets, darting your eyes around the room, and stumbling over basic questions like *"What do you plan to use the funds for?"*, you are signaling uncertainty.

Lenders don't fund uncertainty.

If you can't clearly explain:

- what your business does

- who your customers are

- who you are and your level of experience

- how much money or credit you need

- what you need the money or credit for

- and your plan of repayment

then, unfortunately, you're not ready to apply. Confidence isn't arrogance. It's preparation. The more prepared you are, the smoother the application feels, for you and for the lender. New entrepreneurs often rush into applying because they're excited. Experienced entrepreneurs take their time. They verify their credit profile. They check for errors. They monitor their score. They wait until their foundation is clean and strong before submitting anything.

And when they do apply, they follow one rule religiously: **no more than one or at most two applications per month.**

Every application triggers a hard inquiry. Too many new inquiries (three or more in a single month) appear on your credit profiles, and lenders start to wonder what's going on and why you're scrambling for money. Even if you aren't, the pattern suggests financial stress. Slow, steady application pacing protects your profile and improves your approval odds.

Finally, you must apply for credit cards and loans that match your profile. Do not apply for a premium card if your score isn't strong enough. Don't chase a rewards card if your business is too new. And don't apply for a high-limit product unless your financials support it. Every lender publishes eligibility criteria for a reason. Ignoring them leads to denials, and denials cost you six months of lost opportunity.

The entire purpose of this section is to illustrate that approval begins long before you press the "submit" button.

When your documents are ready, your information is accurate, your application is complete, and your presentation is confident, you will look like a business person worth approving.

Choosing the Right Business Credit Cards: Strategy, Discipline, and Avoiding Costly Mistakes

Once your paperwork is clean, your business identity is consistent on all credit reports showing a business street address, and your or your CFO's credit profile is showing a minimum **720 FICO mid-score or above** on all three credit bureaus, you're finally ready to choose the actual line of credit or business credit cards that will work best for you. Choosing wisely matters far more than people realize. The card itself is not the goal. The goal is what the card does for your business credit, your cash flow, and your long-term financial options.

The first rule of choosing business credit cards is simple: **Apply only for cards that report to Business Experian® Reporting.**

If a card doesn't report to **Experian®**, it doesn't help your business credit foundation. You're using the card, paying it, maintaining good habits, but none of that activity builds the financial reputation lenders care about. Reporting is the difference between simply *using* credit and *building* credit. Too many entrepreneurs choose cards that offer good rewards but do not report to the right bureau, and then wonder why their business credit profile is still thin a year later.

The second rule is just as important: **Choose cards that match your current financial reality, not your future fantasy.**

If your credit score isn't strong enough for a top-tier card, don't apply for it. If the lender clearly states a minimum credit score or revenue requirement, take it seriously. A denial is far more damaging than waiting a few months to strengthen your profile and then applying.

Remember, every denial sits on your consumer report for a minimum of six months. During those six months, lenders see the inquiry, and when the card doesn't appear on your credit report? It doesn't take a rocket scientist to determine you were rejected by that bank. That weakens your future applications. It signals potential risk. And it slows down your progress in building business credit.

Choosing the right card requires more than comparing bonuses. You should look at the introductory APR, long-term APR, cash back structure, reward categories, and whether the benefits actually match the way your business spends money. For example:

- If you travel often, a mileage rewards card makes sense.

- If you buy inventory regularly, a cash back card with high everyday rewards may work better.

- If you need breathing room on cash flow, a zero-percent introductory APR becomes valuable.

A card should fit your business the way a tool fits your hand. You don't buy a hammer because it looks shiny; you buy it because you need to drive a nail. Business credit works the same way.

Now let's talk about the cards themselves. In this chapter, I have listed 10 strong options, each of which reports to **Business Experian®.** These are cards that build your credit history month after month, as long as you use them responsibly. Some have rewards, some have low intro rates, some have bonus categories, and some simply offer predictable credit limit increases. There is no "best" card overall; there is only the card that fits your business profile.

Take the **Chase Ink Business Cash®** card. It's straightforward, offers cash back, and has no annual fee. For many new businesses, a simple card with reliable rewards and strong reporting is exactly what they need. The same goes for **Capital One Spark Cash Select®** and **Bank of America's Business Advantage Cash Rewards®.** These cards don't try to be fancy; they build your credit while giving you practical benefits.

Then you have **American Express®.** This company deserves its own paragraph because it operates differently. **American Express®** is the heavyweight champion of business credit cards. Getting approved for any **AmEx®** business product instantly strengthens your profile, because lenders view **AmEx®** as a premium indicator. Their underwriting standards are strict. Their data is trusted. **American Express®** clients are monitored closely.

But with that strength comes a warning:

If you default on American Express, that mishap becomes an ELE … an extinction-level event.

You don't come back from it. They don't forget. They don't forgive. And no bank will want to deal with a company that burned **AmEx®**. So if you apply, be certain you can handle the responsibility and make your payments on time. It's a privileged card and can do your business a lot of good; however, it certainly is not a starter card. If you manage an **AmEx®** account responsibly, it becomes a powerful asset. But if you ever default, even once, you're finished with them. They don't "reconsider" later. Their computers possess some of the largest data banks in the world, and their memory spans many decades. A default with **American Express®** follows your business like a shadow, and lenders know it. Treat that card with absolute discipline, or you will never carry the card again, and your credit reputation will pay the price.

Other cards, like the **Wells Fargo Business Platinum®, CitiBusiness AAdvantage Platinum Select®,** and **TD Business Solutions Credit Card®,** offer their own unique benefits. They are solid options, especially if you have existing relationships with those banks.

Remember: Lenders love existing customers. If you already have a business checking account with a bank, you have a slight advantage when applying for their credit products. Banks prefer borrowers whose financial activity they can already observe in-house. That makes your approval more likely.

Now, here is something most business credit card guides will never tell you: **The business credit cards you choose affect your future loan approvals.**

Banks look at how you use your existing credit before deciding to extend more credit. If you consistently pay early, keep your utilization low, and handle moderate activity responsibly, lenders see that. They reward it. Credit behavior builds trust, and trust turns into higher limits and eventually business loans.

But if you choose a card with benefits you don't actually use, or one with a high APR that traps you when cash flow gets tight, you're not helping yourself. You're building stress instead of stability. A credit card should never dictate your business behavior. It should support it.

Let's also address something many entrepreneurs get wrong: **Applying for every "good card" you see is a mistake.**

You don't need a deck of credit cards. You need one or two solid, well-managed cards that strengthen your credit profile. When lenders see too many revolving accounts too quickly, they don't think you're strategic. They think of you as a potentially high-risk-of-default business client. And remember, high-risk applicants don't get past the bank's computer approval guidelines.

This section is about setting you up to choose your business credit cards carefully, intentionally, and always with the long game in mind. The cards you select today influence the approvals you will receive later, including the major unsecured business credit lines and loans that we will cover next.

You want cards that strengthen your foundation, not complicate it.

Building Toward Bigger Approvals: Loans, Limits, and the Discipline That Gets You Funded

Business credit cards are only the first step. Once you've established a clean profile with disciplined usage and consistent reporting, you're ready to move into the major leagues of business financing: loans and higher-limit credit products. These are the tools that help you scale, buy equipment, smooth out cash flow, expand operations, or seize opportunities that require serious capital. But banks don't hand out loans because you "want one." They approve borrowers who show stability, structure, and consistency.

Before applying for any loan, step back and understand how lenders think. Business lending is risk management. A bank wants to extend credit, yes, but only to businesses that demonstrate predictable behavior and will pay it back.

They're asking themselves:

If we give this borrower money, will they be able to pay it back on time, with interest, without stress, without excuses, and without putting us in a bad spot with our bosses, regulators, and upper management?

Everything you've built so far, vendor history, **Experian®** Reporting accounts, early payments, low utilization, accurate accounting documents, and clean applications, answers that question before you even meet the banker. When your business foundation is strong, the business loan conversation becomes easier, cleaner, and far more favorable.

I've said this before, but it's worth repeating …

Before applying for a business loan, gather the same documentation you prepared for credit cards, plus anything related to your financials: revenue summaries, profit/loss statements, balance sheet, and three months of your business bank statements.

The potential lender wants a sense of direction, your market, your growth plan, your use of funds, and your repayment plan. They're not looking for a Wall Street pitch deck. They're looking for competence and business stability. A lender who feels confident in your ability to manage credit will say yes far quicker than one who senses uncertainty, disorganization, or financial stress.

You will also see better approval success when your banking relationship has already been established. If you have a business checking account with a bank, they've been quietly observing your behavior, average balances, deposit patterns, activity levels, overdrafts, and consistency. Banks prefer lending to customers whose financial habits they can verify internally. It reduces their risk. So if you're planning to apply for a loan, it's wise to maintain a business checking account with the institution you plan to borrow from.

Let's address the common mistakes business applicants make when evaluating and applying for business loans:

Mistake #1: Applying for the wrong products.

Just like a credit card, simply because a loan product exists doesn't mean you qualify for it. Some loans require specific revenue thresholds. Others require time in business. Others require stronger personal credit. If you ignore eligibility criteria, you're setting yourself up for denials. And as discussed earlier, denials create six months of visibility on your consumer report.

Mistake #2: Asking for too much too soon.

Lenders respect ambition, but they reward realism. Asking for a limit or loan amount far beyond your current profile signals inexperience. They want borrowers who understand their own financial capacity.

Mistake #3: Poor explanations for the use of funds.

If you can't clearly articulate why you need the money, equipment purchase, inventory expansion, seasonal cash flow, marketing and advertising push, then lenders assume you're unprepared and a potential risk. The clearer and more specific your reasoning, the more confident the bank feels.

Now let's talk about one of the strongest signals of reliability: **borrower behavior after approval.**

Your behavior with your first credit card or first business credit line sets the tone. If you keep utilization low, pay early, and manage the line strategically, lenders take notice. A well-managed small line of business credit often leads to larger credit lines automatically as banks review your history.

Here is another key factor: your **debt-to-credit ratio (DTC).** This ratio compares how much revolving debt you carry to the total amount of credit available to you. The lower the ratio, the healthier your credit profile looks. When you apply for a loan, your DTC tells lenders whether you're stretched thin or managing your credit well.

IMPORTANT: Your DTC ratio must be at 30 percent or below before you even think about applying for a business loan.

Borrowers with low ratios get better terms, higher limits, and faster approvals. Borrowers who make the mistake of applying for a business loan with a debt-to-credit ratio above 30 percent will be handed their hat and shown to the door.

Now we come to the second half of this chapter: the list of recommended business credit cards that report to **Business Experian®.** These cards are valuable because they create the kind of reporting banks want to see. They help you strengthen your financial identity far faster than vendor accounts alone. Each card on the list serves a different type of business:

- **Chase Ink Business Cash™**: steady cash back, no annual fee, simple structure

- **AmEx Blue Business Cash™**: one of the strongest foundational cards available

- **Capital One Spark Cash Select™**: fast reporting, easy to manage

- **Wells Fargo Business Platinum™**: solid intro APR for new borrowers

- **CitiBusiness AAdvantage Platinum Select™**: strong for travel-heavy companies

- **Bank of America Business Advantage Cash Rewards™**: category-based rewards

- **Discover it Business™**: flexible categories and friendly reporting

- **US Bank Business Platinum™**: excellent introductory APR

- **PNC Cash Rewards Visa Business™**: consistent reporting

- **TD Business Solutions™**: reward points with no annual fee

These options work because they build credible business credit while giving you financial flexibility. They're not just credit cards.

They're tools. Used correctly, they become stepping stones toward the larger unsecured lines and term loans you will qualify for later.

As you progress from small credit lines to major loans, your job is simple: **Don't do anything that makes a lender second-guess your reliability.** Keep your business information current. Pay all your business and personal bills early. Maintain low utilization. Avoid unnecessary applications. Build relationships. And present yourself and your business confidently every time you apply.

When you manage your credit strategically, you stop hoping for approvals and start *qualifying* for them. Lenders respond to businesses that demonstrate discipline and stability. When you show those qualities, funding opportunities no longer feel difficult; they feel predictable.

Chapter 12

Expanding Your Business Credit Profile

"Bills travel through the mail at twice the speed of checks."

—Steven Wright

At some point, every business reaches a crossroads. You have credit. You've proven you can manage it. Payments are on time, accounts are clean, and lenders are comfortable extending you modest limits. That's a good place to be, but it's not where growth happens. Growth happens when you move beyond basic credit access and start expanding your business credit profile intentionally. This chapter is about that transition: going from having credit to *using credit as a strategic asset.*

Expanding your business credit profile is not about collecting accounts for the sake of it. It's about increasing flexibility, reducing risk, and positioning your company so capital is available when you need it, not when you're desperate. Businesses that survive downturns, seize opportunities, and scale smoothly almost always have one thing in common: access to multiple sources of credit.

The first and most obvious benefit of expanding your credit profile is increased available credit. More available credit gives you breathing room. It allows you to manage cash flow gaps, cover unexpected expenses, and act quickly when opportunities appear.

Cash flow problems rarely come from a lack of revenue; they come from timing. Credit bridges timing gaps. When used correctly, it prevents small issues from turning into major problems.

Beyond flexibility, expanding your credit profile strengthens your business identity. Each additional corporate line of credit, used responsibly, adds depth to your credit file. Lenders don't just look at whether you pay on time; they look at how many obligations you manage successfully. A business that handles multiple accounts responsibly looks far more credible than one with a single credit line and nothing else. Depth matters.

Another often-overlooked benefit is diversification. Credit mix plays a role in how lenders evaluate risk. A profile that includes revolving credit, term credit, and other financial instruments looks more stable than one built around a single type of account. It shows lenders you can manage different obligations simultaneously. That ability translates into trust, and trust translates into better offers and lower interest rates down the line.

As your credit profile strengthens, your terms improve. Lenders reward consistency. Businesses with clean payment histories and diversified credit profiles are offered lower interest rates, higher limits, and longer repayment periods. Over time, this saves you real money. A one or two-point reduction in interest may not sound dramatic, but over the years and across multiple accounts, it adds up fast. Strong credit doesn't just unlock funding; it reduces the cost of using it.

Access to capital is another major reason to expand. Lines of credit give you options. You don't have to use them, but having them available changes how you operate. You can invest in equipment, expand inventory, hire staff, or weather seasonal slowdowns without scrambling. Businesses with access to capital operate from a position of control. Businesses without it operate reactively. One grows; the other survives.

Expanding your credit profile also deepens your relationships with lenders. Banks and financial institutions don't view lending as a one-off transaction. They look for long-term customers. When you open additional credit lines and manage them responsibly, you're building a track record. Over time, lenders become more willing to work with you, restructure terms, increase limits, and offer products that aren't available to first-time borrowers. Relationships matter in finance, and credit is how those relationships are built.

There is also an element of protection involved. Multiple credit lines act as a safety net. If one source tightens terms or reduces availability, you're not exposed. You have alternatives. That redundancy is critical, especially during economic shifts when lenders change policies with little warning. Businesses that rely on a single line of credit are far more vulnerable than those with diversified access.

Your reputation benefits as well. Credit history doesn't exist in a vacuum. Suppliers, lenders, and partners all draw conclusions from how you manage your obligations. A business known for paying early, honoring terms, and managing multiple accounts responsibly earns credibility. That credibility often leads to better vendor terms, smoother negotiations, and unexpected opportunities. People want to do business with companies that look stable.

Expansion also supports growth directly. Whether you're buying equipment, leasing vehicles, adding locations, or scaling operations, credit provides leverage. Growth almost always requires upfront investment. Credit allows you to make those investments without draining operating cash or stalling momentum. The key is having the credit available *before* you need it.

Finally, expanded credit gives you flexibility. Markets change. Opportunities appear without warning. Equipment fails. Clients pay late. When your business has access to capital, these events become manageable instead of catastrophic. Flexibility is not about borrowing more; it's about having options.

Everything in this section leads to one central idea: **Expanding your business credit profile is about control.** Control over timing. Control over growth. Control over risk. Control over your company's future.

As we move through this chapter, we'll cover specific methods for expanding credit responsibly; adding corporate lines, equipment and vehicle leasing; building deeper institutional relationships; and maintaining a payment history that keeps every door open. The goal is not reckless expansion. The goal is *intentional* expansion that strengthens your business instead of burdening it.

If you build credit slowly, thoughtfully, and with discipline, it becomes one of the most powerful tools you have. And when the right opportunity shows up, and it always does, you will be ready to act instead of watching it pass by.

Expanding Business Through Corporate Lines of Credit Without Losing Control

Once you understand why expanding your business credit profile matters, the next step is knowing *how* to do it without creating unnecessary risk. Corporate lines of credit are one of the most effective tools for expansion, but only when they're used with discipline. When used carelessly, they become a burden. When used strategically, they become leverage.

A corporate line of credit increases your available capital without forcing you to take on long-term debt immediately. Unlike term loans, you draw from a line only when you need it. That flexibility is what makes lines of credit so valuable for managing cash flow. Revenue rarely arrives in perfect alignment with expenses. A line of credit smooths those gaps, allowing you to operate consistently even when timing works against you.

Another advantage is credit profile growth. Each well-managed line adds depth to your business credit file. Lenders don't just want to see that you can pay one obligation; they want to see that you can juggle multiple responsibilities without slipping. A business that manages several credit lines cleanly signals to lenders maturity and stability. That signal leads to better opportunities later.

Diversification is another key benefit. Credit profiles that include a mix of revolving lines and other financial products appear less risky than profiles built around a single account. This diversity demonstrates that your business can adapt to different financial obligations. Over time, that adaptability translates into higher trust from lenders and suppliers alike.

Better credit terms follow naturally. Lenders reward behavior. Businesses that maintain low utilization, pay early, and communicate clearly are often offered higher limits and lower interest rates. Those improvements don't happen overnight, but they do compound. Over time, the cost of capital drops while access increases.

Corporate lines of credit also function as a buffer. Unexpected expenses happen. Equipment fails. Clients delay payments. A line of credit gives you room to maneuver without resorting to panic decisions. It protects your cash reserves and helps you avoid missed payments that could damage your credit.

Equally important is relationship-building. Every approved line strengthens your relationship with a financial institution. Banks want repeat borrowers who perform well. When you manage a line responsibly, you become a preferred customer. That status opens doors to additional services, faster approvals, and more flexible terms in the future.

There is also a reputation benefit. Businesses that maintain clean credit profiles across multiple accounts develop a reputation for reliability. That reputation extends beyond banks. Vendors, suppliers, and partners notice it too. Reliable businesses get better terms and more flexibility because trust reduces perceived risk.

A word of advice here… take it slow and easy.

Expanding too quickly is one of the most common mistakes business owners make. Just because you *can* open multiple lines doesn't mean you necessarily *should*. Each new credit line requires management. Each line creates an obligation. Expansion should be paced. A controlled increase, one new line at a time, allows you to maintain visibility and control.

Another mistake is using lines of credit as operating income. I personally have a young friend who hasn't learned this yet, and I worry about him. Lines are tools, not revenue. If your business relies on borrowed funds to cover routine expenses month after month, that's literally a house of cards. It won't last. Lines of credit should support operations, not replace healthy cash flow.

Application discipline matters as well. Just as with credit cards, you should limit applications for lines of credit to one or two per month at most. Multiple inquiries in a short period make lenders uneasy. Slow, deliberate expansion protects your profile and increases approval odds. When applying, choose lenders that align with your business at the time of application. Community banks, regional institutions, and credit unions often offer more flexible underwriting for growing businesses than large national banks. Relationships matter here. A banker who understands your business is more likely to advocate for you during underwriting.

Documentation remains critical. Clean financials, accurate records, and consistent information across all platforms reduce friction. Lenders want clarity. If your numbers make sense and your story is consistent, approvals come easier.

Once approved, how you manage the line determines its long-term value. Keep utilization reasonable. Pay early when possible. **Avoid maxing out the line unless there is a strategic reason; there are some good reasons, like wanting to demonstrate the need for an increased credit line by charging your card up to the limit and then paying it off in full every month.** Communicate with your lender if something changes. Silence creates concern; transparency builds trust.

Used correctly, corporate lines of credit provide more than funding. They provide flexibility, stability, and credibility. They help you grow without stretching yourself thin. They protect you during downturns and empower you during growth phases.

The goal is not to simply accumulate debt, it's to build options. Options give you control, and control is what separates businesses that survive from those that thrive.

As we move forward, we'll look at another powerful expansion tool: leasing equipment and vehicles. Leasing allows you to grow your business without draining cash or overloading your credit, making it an ideal complement to corporate lines of credit.

Using Equipment and Vehicle Leasing to Expand Without Straining Cash or Credit

As your business grows, there comes a point where credit cards and revolving lines alone are no longer enough. You need assets, equipment, vehicles, machinery, and technology to operate efficiently and stay competitive. This is where many business owners make an expensive mistake: they buy everything outright or finance large purchases through traditional loans when leasing would have been the smarter move.

Leasing is not a fallback option. Used correctly, it is a strategic tool that allows you to expand capacity without draining cash, overloading your credit profile, or taking on unnecessary long-term debt.

One of the biggest advantages of leasing is **cash flow preservation**. Purchasing equipment outright ties up large amounts of capital in assets that begin depreciating the moment you put them into service. Leasing spreads that cost into predictable monthly payments, allowing you to keep cash available for operations, marketing, payroll, and growth. Businesses rarely fail because they lack assets; they fail because they run out of liquidity. Leasing helps prevent that.

Leasing also supports **credit expansion without pressure**. Many leasing companies report activity differently from traditional lenders, and some do not require heavy utilization of your existing credit lines. That means you can add operational capacity without maxing out revolving accounts or triggering concern from banks. In many cases, leasing preserves your core credit lines for opportunities where flexibility matters most.

There are also **tax advantages** to leasing. In many situations, lease payments are deductible as operating expenses, which can reduce taxable income. While you should always confirm specifics with your accountant, leasing often provides cleaner tax treatment than depreciation schedules tied to ownership. That simplicity alone can be valuable for growing companies.

Another major benefit is **predictability**. Lease payments are fixed. You know exactly what you owe each month. That makes cash flow forecasting far easier than dealing with repair spikes or replacement costs, or financing balloon payments. Predictability allows you to plan confidently instead of reacting to surprises.

Maintenance is another overlooked factor. Many leases include maintenance and service packages. When equipment breaks down, you're not scrambling to cover repair bills or dealing with downtime alone. This reduces operational risk and keeps your business running smoothly. For vehicle fleets especially, maintenance-inclusive leases can save substantial time and money.

Leasing also provides **access to newer equipment**. Technology evolves quickly. Owning outdated equipment can slow you down, reduce efficiency, and make you less competitive. Leasing allows you to upgrade at the end of the term instead of being stuck with aging assets. Staying current is not about appearances; it's about performance.

Risk management is another reason experienced operators favor leasing. When you own an asset, you assume all the residual risk. When it becomes obsolete, damaged, or unwanted, disposal becomes your problem. Leasing transfers much of that risk to the leasing company. At the end of the term, you return the asset, upgrade, or renegotiate. That flexibility matters when markets shift.

Leasing also helps preserve your **corporate credit lines**. Because many leases do not require large down payments or traditional collateral, they allow you to grow without tapping into your revolving credit. That leaves your lines available for inventory, expansion, or unexpected needs. Smart businesses don't burn their best credit on depreciating assets.

That said, leasing is not an automatic approval territory. Leasing companies still evaluate your business. They look at time in business, revenue stability, and credit behavior. Clean payment history matters. So does consistency. The stronger your business credit profile, the better your lease terms will be.

This is where discipline pays off. Businesses that pay vendors early, keep utilization low, and manage multiple accounts responsibly are viewed as lower risk. Lower risk translates into better lease rates, more flexible terms, and easier approvals. Leasing rewards good credit behavior just as much as traditional lending does.

Another important point: **Leasing should align with actual business needs**. Do not lease equipment simply because approval is easy. Every lease creates an obligation. The asset must generate value. If it does not increase efficiency, revenue, or operational stability, it becomes a liability instead of a tool.

Choose lease terms carefully. Shorter terms often cost more per month but provide flexibility. Longer terms reduce monthly payments but increase total cost. Neither option is "better" universally. The right choice depends on how long the equipment will remain productive for your business.

Leasing vehicles deserves special mention. For many businesses, vehicles are essential but expensive. Leasing allows you to maintain a reliable fleet without large capital outlays. It also simplifies upgrades, branding, and maintenance. When structured correctly, vehicle leases can support expansion without stressing your balance sheet.

Used properly, leasing complements corporate credit lines perfectly. Lines handle cash flow and flexibility. Leases handle capacity and assets. Together, they allow you to scale intelligently instead of aggressively.

The key takeaway is simple: **Expansion does not require ownership. It requires control.** Leasing gives you control over your cash retention, risk, and financial growth without forcing you into cash-intensive permanent financial commitments.

Strengthening Your Credit Through Banking Relationships and Payment Discipline

Expanding your business credit profile is not just about opening more accounts. It is about building a reputation, one that follows your business quietly but powerfully. That reputation is shaped by two things more than anything else: the relationships you build with financial institutions and the payment habits you maintain over time.

Credit products open doors, but personal and business relationships decide how wide those doors open and how long they stay that way.

Let's start with financial institutions. Banks, credit unions, and lenders are not vending machines. You don't insert an application and wait for credit to fall out. They are relationship-driven organizations, even when the process feels automated. Behind every approval is a person who has to justify that decision to someone else. The stronger your relationship, the easier that justification becomes.

The first step in building these relationships is understanding your own business needs. You should know exactly what you're looking for before you ever sit down with a banker. Are you seeking revolving credit, term loans, equipment financing, treasury services, or long-term growth capital? Clarity matters. When you know what you need, bankers can help you structure the right solutions instead of guessing.

Research matters as well. Not every financial institution is right for every business. Some specialize in certain industries. Some prefer established companies. Others work well with growing firms. Look for institutions with a strong track record serving businesses like yours. Reputation matters on both sides of the table.

Networking plays a role here, but not in the superficial way people often imagine. Attending industry events, conferences, and local business gatherings at your Chamber of Commerce gives you access to decision-makers you would never reach through an online application. These interactions build familiarity. Familiarity builds trust. Trust leads to better outcomes when it's time to apply for credit.

Once you identify a banker who understands your industry, invest in that relationship. Schedule meetings. Keep them informed. Share your goals and challenges honestly. Transparency goes a long way in finance. Bankers are impressed by your preparedness, your honesty, and, of course, how successful you and your business become, which makes you a very important client to the bank.

Communication and occasional schmoozing are essential. Keep your banker updated when your business changes, adds new products and new markets, and especially when there is increased revenue and business expansion plans. Regular communication keeps you top of his or her mind. When opportunities arise inside the institution, bankers think first of their best clients that they know and trust.

Follow-through is non-negotiable. If you promise to provide documents by a certain date, deliver them by the date promised. This is extremely important. Missed commitments damage credibility faster than almost anything else. Reliability is the currency of finance. Every time you follow through, you add to your credibility bank.

As relationships deepen, opportunities expand. Financial institutions often offer services beyond credit: insurance products, investment services, treasury management, and advisory support. Exploring these services strengthens the relationship and integrates your business more deeply into the institution. Integrated clients are viewed as lower risk and higher value. You might also consider joining your local Chamber of Commerce. You can make a lot of solid business contacts and form business relationships. If you would like to learn more about this subject, I would suggest calling the Beverly Hills offices of the Wilshire Financial Group **at**

1-888-383-5318 and asking to speak directly with our Chamber of Commerce Ambassador, Mr. Cesar Osorio. He has a wealth of knowledge concerning this topic.

Now let's talk about the other side of expansion: **payment history**. No relationship survives poor payment behavior. Maintaining a strong corporate payment history is the single most powerful way to protect and expand your credit profile. Everything we've discussed, credit lines, leases, relationships, rests on this foundation.

Consistent on-time payments build your business credit score. Lenders use that score as a shorthand for trustworthiness. A strong score increases approval odds and improves terms. A weak score does the opposite. There is no shortcut here. Payment history is earned, not negotiated.

Good payment behavior also increases future access to credit. Lenders prefer borrowers with a proven track record. When they see consistent early or on-time payments, they feel comfortable extending additional credit. That comfort translates into higher limits and more flexible terms.

Better payment history improves pricing. Interest rates drop. Fees decrease. Repayment terms lengthen. Over time, these improvements save substantial money. Late payments, on the other hand, cost far more than most business owners realize. Penalties, higher rates, reduced limits, and damaged relationships all stem from missed or late payments.

Cash flow management plays a role here. Paying on time requires planning. Businesses that track obligations carefully avoid surprises.

This discipline protects your reputation and reduces stress. When payments are predictable, your business operates smoothly.

Reputation extends beyond lenders. Vendors and suppliers pay attention to payment behavior. Businesses known for paying reliably are offered better terms and flexibility. Those benefits often outweigh minor price differences. Trust creates options.

Strong payment history also reduces default risk. Defaults damage credit profiles for years. Avoiding them protects your future borrowing power. Paying attention to obligations today prevents painful consequences tomorrow.

There is also an intangible benefit: peace of mind. Businesses with clean payment histories sleep better. Owners can focus on growth instead of worrying about credit damage or financial fallout. That clarity improves decision-making across the board.

Long-term relationships grow out of consistent behavior. Lenders and suppliers prefer working with businesses they can rely on. Those relationships often lead to unexpected opportunities, faster approvals, special programs, or favorable terms not advertised publicly.

The takeaway from this section is straightforward: **Credit expansion succeeds when solid relationships and discipline work together.** Opening accounts without managing them carefully leads to trouble. Managing accounts without building good relationships limits opportunity. When both are present, your business credit profile becomes a strategic asset.

This chapter completes the transition from building credit to *leveraging* it. You now understand how to expand responsibly, protect flexibility, and strengthen credibility. Used wisely, business credit becomes one of the most powerful tools you have for growth, stability, and long-term success.

158

Chapter 13

Personal Guarantees: How They Can Affect Your Business and Your Credit

"Procrastination is like a credit card: it's a lot of fun until you get the bill."

—Christopher Parker

A personal guarantee is one of those things that sounds harmless until you understand what it actually does. On the surface, it feels like a formality, just another signature on a loan document to get the deal done. In reality, it is a legally binding promise that can reach straight past your business and into your personal life. If you don't understand it fully, a personal guarantee can undo years of careful planning in a single bad decision.

At its core, a personal guarantee means this: If the business does not pay the debt, **you** are personally responsible. Depending upon the type of loan you agree to co-sign, that responsibility may extend to personal assets such as savings, investments, wages, and in some cases, even your home. This is true whether you are guaranteeing debt for your own business or acting as a CFO or credit partner for someone else's company.

This is why I am very direct about one thing right out of the gate: **You must understand exactly what kind of loan you are applying for before you even think about agreeing to sign a personal guarantee.**

If you are applying strictly for unsecured, stated-income business credit, the risk profile is very different than if you are guaranteeing a secured business loan. **Secured loans are backed by collateral.** When things go wrong, and sometimes they do, that collateral can include personal assets. For that reason alone, I strongly advise against personally guaranteeing any secured business loan unless you have given it considerable thought. The downside is simply too large.

Lenders require personal guarantees for one reason: risk reduction. When a business is small or relatively young, lenders want an extra layer of protection. A personal guarantee tells the lender that if the business struggles, someone with a personal balance sheet is still on the hook. From the lender's perspective, it makes perfect sense. However, you have the final decision. Remember this: What a lender might want doesn't necessarily mean they get it. This is where you negotiate or change the loan structure of your application.

There are generally three types of personal guarantees. An **unlimited personal guarantee** makes you responsible for the entire debt, no matter how large it becomes. A **limited personal guarantee** caps your responsibility at a specific amount or percentage. A **stated income loan guarantee** means all that is at risk is your personal credit rating, not your physical assets. Many borrowers don't realize there is a difference, and even fewer attempt to negotiate it. Don't make this mistake. Terms are often negotiable, especially if the business is otherwise strong.

One of the most misunderstood aspects of personal guarantees is how they affect your personal credit. Here is the truth:

As long as the business pays on time, a personal guarantee does **nothing** to your consumer credit. It is a neutral event. It stays under the radar. The credit bureaus do not reward you for guaranteeing debt, and they do not penalize you unless something goes wrong.

But if something does go wrong—late payments, defaults, judgments, and charge-offs—say goodbye to your excellent credit rating. That damage will follow you around for at least seven years. It will significantly lower your personal consumer credit score and make future borrowing far more expensive and much more difficult. That is why confidence in the business matters, and your risk vs. reward must be taken into consideration. If you do not fully trust the business model or the person running the operation, you should not be offering your personal credit as backup. Run away, don't walk.

Your business structure plays a major role here. Corporations and LLCs exist specifically to limit personal liability. When structured and operated correctly, they provide a layer of separation between business obligations and your personal assets. Understanding how to use that structure properly is one of the primary reasons this book exists. Many business owners lose the protection they could have had simply because they didn't know how to set things up correctly.

So what are the alternatives? Truly unsecured business loans without personal guarantees are rare. They exist, but they are not common. Lines of credit without guarantees are even rarer. That said, **guarantees are often negotiable.** You may be able to limit the amount, shorten the duration, or substitute collateral instead. These conversations don't happen unless you ask. Silence always favors the lender.

Before agreeing to any personal guarantee, legal advice is worth considering. I'll be honest, I am not a fan of lawyers. I've paid them more money than I care to remember. From my experiences, they have killed more deals than they have saved. That said, when the law is involved, and your personal exposure is real, they can be a necessary evil.

If you hire a lawyer, the most important advice I can give you is … to listen to them. Follow their advice. And be prepared to pay the piper. Good legal guidance is rarely inexpensive, but ignorance is far more expensive.

This section is not meant to scare you. It is meant to slow you down just enough to make a clear-headed decision. A personal guarantee is not automatically bad. Sometimes it is the right move and can be very profitable. But it should never be casual, rushed into, or misunderstood.

How to Mitigate Risk When You Decide to Guarantee Business Debt Personally

Once you understand what a personal guarantee actually means, the next question becomes practical rather than theoretical: *How do you protect yourself if you decide to sign one anyway?* Because the truth is, despite all the warnings, there are situations where a personal guarantee is unavoidable. The key is making sure the risk is calculated, contained, and managed, not blind.

The first layer of risk mitigation starts **before** you sign anything. This means understanding the deal in plain English, not lender language. You need to know exactly what you are guaranteeing, for how long, and under what conditions your obligation is triggered. Many guarantees are written broadly on purpose. If you don't ask questions, you may be agreeing to far more exposure than you realize.

One of the most important distinctions is whether the guarantee is **limited or unlimited**. An unlimited guarantee gives the lender full recourse against you for the entire balance, interest, fees, and legal costs. A limited guarantee caps your exposure. If there is any opportunity to limit the amount, duration, or scope of the guarantee, you should pursue it. Lenders won't volunteer this option, but it often exists, especially if the business has other strengths.

Another critical step is understanding **what type of loan** you are guaranteeing. Secured business loans represent the highest personal risk. These loans are tied to collateral, and when combined with a personal guarantee, they can put personal assets directly in harm's way. In my opinion, personally guaranteeing secured business debt is one of the most dangerous positions you can put yourself in. The downside is not worth it. If the business fails, you lose twice, once through the business and again personally.

Unsecured stated-income business loans are different. While they still carry risk, they do not automatically place liens on personal property. That difference matters. Knowing where the boundary lies is essential.

Communication is another form of protection. If you are guaranteeing debt for a business, your own or someone else's, you should never operate in the dark. You must stay informed. That means regular updates on cash flow, expenses, and payment status. Silence is dangerous. Problems don't appear overnight; they build quietly. The earlier you know about trouble, the more options you have.

Monitoring your personal credit is non-negotiable. A personal guarantee may be neutral while everything is going well, but the moment something slips, your personal credit becomes the canary in the coal mine. Regular monitoring allows you to catch issues early, before they become defaults, judgments, or collections.

If you are acting as a CFO or credit partner for another business, the standard must be even higher. You are putting your personal financial reputation on the line for someone else's decisions. In that situation, trust is not enough. You need visibility, access, and authority. If you cannot see the books, influence financial decisions, intervene when necessary, or have a substantial payments reserve account set up by the borrower for your protection, where you have access to monitor the balance, then you should not be guaranteeing the debt.

There are also contractual protections you can insist on. One of the most effective and least known protections is requiring **written notification of missed payments**. You can do this directly on the loan agreement. By clearly stating that you must be notified in writing within a specific time frame of any missed payment, you create a legal obligation for the lender. This gives you the opportunity to step in early, before damage spreads.

Following that up with a certified letter restating the requirement creates a paper trail. Keep copies. Keep receipts. These documents are not paranoia; they are insurance. If the lender fails to notify you as agreed, you may have a valid defense against liability or negative reporting. *Banks do not advertise this option,* but it is entirely reasonable and lawful.

Another layer of protection is psychological rather than legal: **Do not co-sign casually**. Never co-sign out of guilt, emotion, or pressure. **That includes family.** Money and relationships rarely mix well, and credit guarantees amplify the damage when things go wrong. If you wouldn't invest your own cash into the business without hesitation, you should not invest your credit.

Finally, be realistic. Even strong businesses can fail due to market shifts, illness, partnerships gone wrong, or external shocks. A personal guarantee assumes best-case behavior under worst-case conditions. If that assumption makes you uncomfortable, listen to that instinct.

Risk mitigation is not about fear. It is about awareness and preparation. A personal guarantee should be a deliberate choice made with full understanding, not a checkbox clicked in a hurry to "get approved." When you treat it seriously, you protect both your business future and your personal financial life.

Co-Signing for Others: When It Makes Sense and When It Absolutely Does Not

There is a big difference between personally guaranteeing debt for your own business and co-signing for someone else's. One is a calculated business decision. The other is a gamble that too often ends badly. Over the years, I've watched intelligent, disciplined people wreck their personal credit, not because they made bad business decisions, but because they trusted the wrong people.

Let's be very clear about this upfront:

Co-signing for someone else is one of the highest-risk financial decisions you can make.

When you co-sign, you are "helping someone get approved." But don't forget you are volunteering to be financially responsible if they fail. The lender does not see you as a backup plan. They see you as a primary payer if things go sideways. And lenders will not hesitate to come after you first if you are easier to collect from.

In my opinion, there is only one situation where co-signing for someone else should even be considered:

When you are well compensated as a CFO or financial partner, and you have full visibility and authority over the business finances or payment reserve account, should the need arise.

That's it

Not for your friends

Not for your relatives

Not long-time acquaintances with "great ideas."

And, not for your adult children

If that sounds harsh, it's because experience has taught me that emotional decisions around credit almost always end in regret. Credit does not care about good intentions. It only cares about on-time payment history.

The most dangerous co-signing situations are the ones that begin with reassurance. Statements like *"It's just temporary, Dad, the car is a real beauty, and I'll never miss a payment,"* or *"The business is just about to take off, making the payments will be a cake walk"* should set off proceed with caution alarms in your head. The people who need co-signers are often the same people who lack the financial discipline to manage debt properly. That doesn't make them bad people. It makes them risky borrowers and unintentional credit destroyers.

When you co-sign, you lose control. You don't control how the money is used. You don't control when payments are made. You don't control cash flow decisions. Yet you absorb the consequences if anything goes wrong. That imbalance alone should make you pause and weigh the risk vs. reward.

If you do decide to co-sign in a professional capacity, you must insist on safeguards. Visibility into bank accounts, monthly financial statements, and real-time payment confirmation is not optional. If you cannot verify that payments are being made on time, you are flying blind. Blind risk is unacceptable.

You must also stay in constant communication. Regular monitoring allows you to react quickly, sometimes quickly enough to prevent permanent damage.

Silence is the enemy. If a borrower stops answering calls or avoids financial conversations, that is often the first sign of trouble, and it's probably already too late. Kiss your excellent credit rating, that took you years to build, goodbye.

Once you've co-signed, early awareness is your only real defense. Once a payment is missed and reported, it's too late. The damage begins immediately.

One of the most valuable protections you can use when co-signing is requiring written notification of missed payments. This should not be a handshake understanding. It should be documented. Written, clear, and enforceable. When done correctly, this requirement forces the lender to notify you early, giving you a chance to intervene before the situation escalates.

If you receive a delinquency notice, action must be immediate. You do not wait. You do not hope it resolves itself. You get on the phone and address the issue directly. Delay is how small problems turn into credit disasters.

Now let me say something that makes some people uncomfortable, but it needs to be said again:

Do not co-sign for family.

Parents ruin their retirement trying to save adult children. Siblings destroy relationships over missed payments. Friendships end over unpaid debt. Credit does not strengthen relationships; it tests them. And most relationships fail that test.

If you want to help someone financially, do it in a way that does not involve your credit. Give advice. Provide education. Even provide limited capital if you can afford to lose it. But once your credit is attached, the stakes change completely.

The reason lenders love co-signers is simple: It shifts risk away from them and onto you. That should tell you everything you need to know.

Co-signing is not generosity. It is a liability. And liability should only be accepted when the reward justifies the risk and when you retain enough control to protect yourself.

This section is not meant to scare you away from every opportunity. It is meant to force honesty. If you are comfortable losing the relationship, the money, and potentially your credit, then you are at least making an informed decision. If that thought makes you uneasy, trust that instinct.

Credit decisions are not emotional decisions. They are risk decisions. And when the risk belongs to you, caution is not weakness; it is intelligence.

Why Personal Guarantees Became Standard and How to Protect Yourself Going Forward

Personal guarantees did not become common by accident. They became standard because lenders learned, often the hard way, that relying solely on business credit profiles was not enough to protect them from widespread risk. To understand why guarantees are now baked into most small business lending, you have to look back at what changed the banking system permanently.

Three words explain it: **the subprime meltdown**.

Between 2007 and 2010, the American financial system took a hit that reshaped lending forever. Banks had spent years extending credit to borrowers who never should have qualified—often through "stated income" loans with little verification and high-interest adjustable rates that were designed and influenced by greedy lenders and, unfortunately, destined to fail. When the housing market collapsed, defaults exploded. Mortgage-backed securities imploded. Liquidity dried up. And banks suddenly realized they had been underwriting risk instead of managing it.

Small businesses were collateral damage.

As banks pulled back, small business lending tightened dramatically. Credit lines vanished. Stated income programs disappeared almost overnight. For a period of time, lending froze entirely. Institutions that had once been aggressive lenders shut their doors or disappeared altogether. The collapse of Washington Mutual

Bank was a wake-up call across the industry. Nobody wanted to be the next headline.

The result was a shift toward **risk automation**. Banks moved lending decisions away from individual loan officers and into computerized underwriting systems. Human discretion gave way to algorithms. You either met the criteria or you didn't. No exceptions, no charm, and no second chances.

This change also altered accountability. Loan officers were no longer willing to stick their necks out. If a loan went bad, it wasn't "their call." The system approved it. But to justify approvals internally, banks needed extra protection. That protection came in the form of personal guarantees.

From a lender's perspective, guarantees solved multiple problems. They reduced losses. They discouraged reckless borrowing. And they aligned incentives. If someone's personal credit was on the line, lenders believed they would behave more responsibly.

Whether that belief is fair is irrelevant. It is the system we now operate in, and it's working.

The good news is that the same automation that made guarantees standard also created predictability. Today, small business loan approvals follow defined criteria. When you meet them, approvals happen quickly. When you don't, the application is rejected just as fast. The chaos of discretionary lending is gone.

Experienced firms adapted.

After the meltdown, organizations that survived learned to work within the new rules. Applications were pre-screened. Credit profiles were cleaned up before submission. Weak points were fixed in advance. When an application went to the bank, it already met the algorithm's requirements.

That is the real lesson here.

Personal guarantees are not going away. But they are no longer a mystery. When you understand why they exist, how they are triggered, and how to limit exposure, they become manageable instead of terrifying.

The key going forward is discipline:

- Structure your business correctly.

- Use business credit strategically.

- Avoid secured loans that require a personal guarantee whenever possible.

- Monitor your credit regularly.

- Communicate early when problems appear.

- Never sign blindly.

- Never co-sign for a loan emotionally.

- And when you do decide to accept personal liability, do so with safeguards in place and eyes wide open.

The biggest mistake business owners make is assuming they can ignore personal guarantees until the moment a lender puts one in front of them. By then, the decision is rushed. Pressure is high. And mistakes happen.

You are now past that stage.

You now understand what a personal guarantee involves, when it matters, and how to protect yourself if you ever sign one. That knowledge alone puts you ahead of most borrowers. Credit does not reward ignorance, but it does reward informed, intelligent decisions.

Handled correctly, personal guarantees become a calculated tool, even a source of passive income as a professional CFO candidate, not a hidden trap. Handled casually, they become the most expensive signature you will ever write.

Chapter 14

What's Happening Now, and How It Will Affect Your Business, Your Credit, and Your Life

"All the armies of Europe, Asia, and Africa combined, with all the treasure of the earth (our own excepted) in their military chest; with a Bonaparte for a commander, could not by force, take a drink from the Ohio, or make a track on the Blue Ridge, in a trial of a thousand years. At what point then is the approach of danger to be expected? I answer. If it ever reach us it must spring up amongst us. It cannot come from abroad. If destruction be our lot, we must ourselves be its author and finisher. As a nation of freemen, we must live through all time, or die by suicide."

—Abraham Lincoln

There is no gentle way to frame this. The environment in which business owners are operating right now is harder than it should be, and much of that difficulty has nothing to do with skill, intelligence, or effort. It comes from distraction. Constant noise and never-ending commentary from a barrage of so called "unbiased" news reporters working day and night, seemingly trying to divide our country. The weapon of choice? Distraction! Using an elementary school playground approach, a childish game of insisting you must pick a team. What's your choice? Pick one … blue or red? Too many people are being sucked into this waste of time, and unfortunately, taking their eye off the ball and the big game. Trying desperately hard to make sense of it all and deciding which team, red or blue, they want to be on.

Ladies and gentlemen, we must mentally silence the talking heads. Turn off the television, the constant political cycles of outrage, and the daily panic being marketed as "news," all screaming "stampede." Every television and radio channel doing their best to rile up the herd.

At this point, one thing should become very clear: We're all Americans. And today, more than any other time in history, we all better be on the same team.

I've been around for a long time, and I have seen a lot of changes, but nothing compares to what is on the horizon. I have come to the realization that today, right now, we're living through the most important and significant time in all of recorded human history and … most people are totally unaware. If I am correct, an imminent pending event will change everything. It is very important, now more than ever, that you begin immediately to take control of your own financial destiny. Don't be distracted from your goal. Stay the course that builds your business, improves your credit, and changes your financial outcome. Time and energy are the two most valuable resources entrepreneurs have and certainly cannot afford to waste.

Successful business owners have always understood: Progress happens when attention, time, and energy are invested in work that compounds success:

Manufacturing

Creating

Selling

Serving consumers

Managing money

Building

Everything else is a waste of time and your energy.

Right now, too many people are sitting still, watching, reacting, commenting, or staring at their phones while opportunities quietly pass them by. Economies don't collapse because people work too hard. They stall when people stop producing, stop working, sit on their hands and wait for the "right time."

This book has been about the need for you to take control of your own financial destiny from the very beginning. Control of your credit. Control of your business structure. Control of your risk. Control of your future. That theme matters even more now. In uncertain times, the people who move forward are not the loudest or the angriest. They are the ones who put their heads down, stay focused, and move forward.

Business owners do not need anyone's permission to act. They don't need perfect economic conditions. They don't need the public consensus. They need discipline and direction. History makes that painfully clear. Every period of economic strain has produced two groups: those who froze and watched and those who adapted, moved forward, and took care of business.

Another hard truth: Consumer-only behavior is a dead end. Sitting back and consuming media, opinions, and entertainment creates dependency. Producing creates leverage. Entrepreneurs who focus on making, building, fixing, exporting, contributing to, and improving the world place themselves on the productive side of the equation. That position carries power, even when conditions are tough. That's exactly when the tough get going.

None of this requires grand speeches or slogans. It requires practical decisions. Tuning out all of the distractions. Getting back to fundamentals. Asking better questions like:

- What problem does my business solve right now?

- What can I produce, improve, or deliver better than last year?

- Where can I tighten operations and still generate additional cash flow?

- How do I position myself so lenders, suppliers, and partners see stability instead of risk when assessing my business?

Those questions lead to action. Action leads to progress. Progress builds confidence, internally and externally. That confidence shows up in credit approvals, customer trust, and long-term resilience.

There is also something deeply personal about this moment. Business ownership has never been easy, but it has always been meaningful. It forces responsibility. It demands effort. It rewards consistency. When distractions pull people away from that responsibility, the cost shows up everywhere: financially, professionally, and personally.

The most dangerous habit right now is sitting on the sidelines waiting. Waiting for conditions to improve. Waiting for world clarity. Waiting for reassurances from someone other than yourself to move forward. And so you continue waiting and waiting and waiting …

Waiting is a very expensive proposition. While you wait, the clock is ticking; others are moving. Markets adjust. Credit standards shift. Opportunities pass you by and close quietly.

Getting back to work doesn't mean ignoring reality. It means refusing to be paralyzed by it. It means focusing on what you can control: your output, your discipline, your preparation. Those things still matter. They always will.

This chapter is not about nostalgia or slogans. It's about posture. Are you positioned as a builder or a spectator? Are you producing value or consuming commentary? One path leads somewhere. The other leads you nowhere.

In every cycle, the businesses that survive and grow are the ones that recommit to fundamentals when others drift. They manufacture solutions. They serve real needs. They export value instead of importing excuses. They focus on execution, not hesitation and explanation.

The good news is simple: **Nothing has changed about what works**. Hard work focused on the projects still works. Discipline still works. Credit still rewards consistency. Lenders still favor preparation and determination. Customers still pay for value.

Noise comes and goes. Focus, persistence, and work produce results and success.

That's where the advantage is right now, just like always.

How This Moment Shapes Your Business, Your Credit, and Your Life

Every economic cycle eventually asks the same question of business owners: *What are you going to do now to make this work?* The answers you give today will always show up later. Opinions and good intentions don't move the ball down the field. Making a decision and taking action does. The survival and success of your business sets you apart from those who choose to sit it out and watch.

What's happening right now affects you and your business. Banks are more cautious. Underwriting models are tighter. Risk tolerance is lower. That doesn't mean opportunity is gone. It means standards matter more. Businesses that are financially prepared, with clean records, consistent payments, and stable operations, stand out more now than ever.

This is where discipline pays dividends. When you pay early instead of on time, lenders notice. When you keep utilization low, algorithms respond. When your business information is accurate and consistent, approvals come easier. None of that is dramatic. However, all of it is effective.

The same applies to life outside the balance sheet. Running a business in turbulent times forces clarity. You become more selective about where your energy goes. You stop listening to all the distracting noise and start investing your time in taking actions that will produce positive outcomes. That shift improves decision-making, reduces stress, and restores a sense of control that many people give away without realizing it.

Good credit is not just a financial tool; it's a reflection of positive behavior and money when you need it. The habits that build strong credit profiles are the same habits that build strong businesses: consistency, follow-through, restraint, and long-term thinking. When those habits are present, your business progress becomes predictable. When they're absent, nothing works for long.

This chapter was written to remind you that none of the fundamentals have changed. The path forward still looks the same:

- Do real work that creates value.

- Manage money carefully.

- Build credit deliberately.

- Avoid shortcuts that create long-term damage.

- Focus on production instead of distraction.

That path is not flashy, but it is reliable.

Business ownership has always rewarded people who move when others hesitate. When conditions feel uncertain, competition thins out. Some people pull back. Many will sit still, wait, and watch. That creates space for those willing to act. Slow and steady disciplined action is one of the greatest competitive advantages available.

The same mindset applies to credit. Many business owners will sit on their hands and avoid applying for the money they need simply because they assume rejection is inevitable. In reality, most rejections come from lack of preparation, not lack of opportunity. When your business credit profile is clean, your business structure is sound, and your behavior is consistent, lenders respond positively, even in tight environments.

Your life improves when your business is stable. Stress decreases. Options expand. Decisions become proactive instead of reactive.

That stability doesn't come from waiting for external conditions to improve. It comes from internal order.

This is where everything in this book connects. Your business structure, the credit bureaus. vendor accounts. corporate credit cards, lines of credit, the guarantees you commit to, and business relationships. None of it exists in isolation. It all feeds one outcome: **financial freedom through advanced preparation, perseverance, persistence, and starting your own business.**

Being prepared does not mean being aggressive. It means being ready. Ready to act when an opportunity appears. Ready to weather a slowdown. Ready to say yes when others can't. That readiness shows up in solid credit files, financial statements, and personal confidence long before anyone else notices.

There is no perfect time to build, expand, or improve. There is only the time you choose to take action and make it work for you. History is full of people who waited too long and missed their window of opportunity. It's also full of people who kept working quietly, persistently, and emerged successful.

The choice remains the same today as it was yesterday, tomorrow, and always will be. Consume noise, become distracted, and sit on your hands, or take action, start today, and create value.

Be so good, so well prepared, so disciplined, and so dedicated and persistent that the results will speak for themselves and ... you cannot be ignored.

Chapter 15

Conclusion

"In any moment of decision, the best thing you can do is the right thing, the next best thing is the wrong thing, and the worst thing you can do is nothing."

—Theodore Roosevelt

Every business failure I've personally witnessed over the last 50 years has had one thing in common. It didn't start with a dramatic collapse. It didn't happen overnight. It began slowly with a good-sized helping of hesitation. With a decision to wait, to delay. With people knowing what needed to be done and then choosing to wait and not move forward.

Doing nothing feels safe. It feels neutral. It feels like you're avoiding risk. In reality, it is the most expensive decision a business owner can make.

Most people understand business credit only as money borrowed. That's a bad mistake. Credit is time. Credit is leverage. Credit is optionality and opportunity. And when you delay building it, structuring it, and using it intelligently, you give all three away.

That's why this book has never been about tricks, shortcuts, or loopholes. It's about the preparation of financial resources. Financial preparation before the need becomes obvious. Financial preparation before conditions tighten. Financial preparation before the doors quietly close and before it is too late.

The world has always rewarded people who plan ahead and take action early. Not reckless action, but action taken thoughtfully, deliberately, and steadily. Waiting for the perfect time has never been a winning strategy. Markets don't pause. Opportunities don't announce themselves with countdown clocks.

The difference between people who succeed and those who struggle is rarely intelligence. It's timing and action.

There is an old cartoon character many readers will remember, "Wimpy," from *Popeye the Sailor Man*. Always smiling, always hungry, and always searching for a burger on credit. His famous line, *"I'll gladly pay you tomorrow for a hamburger today,"* was funny because it was familiar. Everyone knows someone like that.

Now let's substitute "Uncle Sam" for Wimpy.

For decades now, our country has been operating a lot like the cartoon character Wimpy. Spend today. Pay back tomorrow. That pattern works, until it doesn't. And when it stops working, the people least prepared are hit first and the hardest.

Small business owners feel the impact before anyone else. Credit tightens. Costs rise. Consumers pull back and stop spending. Banks hesitate. The environment becomes less forgiving very quickly.

That's why waiting is dangerous.

If you are reading this book, you already understand something many people never grasp: Financial independence is built, not granted. Financial stability doesn't come from headlines, opinions, or commentary. It comes from structure. From discipline, responsibility, and taking action early instead of reacting when it's too late.

Nothing in this book promises certainty. What it offers is control. Control over your credit profile. Control over your funding options. Control over how exposed you are when conditions shift.

The worst position to be in, financially, professionally, personally, is unprepared and surprised. That's what doing nothing produces.

This section is not about fear. It's about honesty. You don't need to panic. You don't need to rush blindly. But you do need to make a decision. Movement matters much more than perfection.

Every chapter before this one has been about equipping you with tools. This chapter is about reminding you why unused tools are meaningless.

Business ownership rewards action taken early and punishes delay taken lightly. That has never changed. It never will.

Doing something, even imperfectly, moves you forward. Doing nothing guarantees you stay exactly where you are.

Independence Is Not a Theory, It's a Decision

There comes a moment for every person who wants control over their future when the conversation shifts from ideas to responsibility. Not responsibility in the abstract sense, but responsibility for your income, your financial stability, and the direction your life takes. That moment does not arrive with fanfare. It usually arrives quietly, when you realize that no institution, employer, or system is going to prioritize your future the way you must.

Financial independence is often misunderstood as only a destination. In reality, it's a posture. It's a way of operating. It begins the moment you stop outsourcing your security to forces you do not control.

Starting or expanding a business is not about chasing money. It's about reclaiming leverage over your life. A business, when structured properly and supported by intelligent credit, gives you options. Options reduce fear. Options allow you to act instead of react. That is what independence actually looks like.

Too many people wait for conditions to feel safe before making a move. Safe rarely arrives on schedule. What does arrive on schedule are your bills, responsibilities, and your obligations that don't pause just because the economic environment is uncertain. Independence is built by people who move even when conditions are unclear, but their advance preparation is solid.

This book has shown you how credit works when it is used as a tool instead of a crutch. Credit, properly managed, gives you room to breathe. It allows you to fund growth, absorb shocks, and take advantage of timing. Used recklessly, it becomes a trap. Used deliberately, it becomes your insulation, safety, and security.

The decision to build a business, or strengthen an existing one, is not a rejection of employment, institutions, or systems. It is an acknowledgment that reliance on anyone other than yourself is a risk. Diversity of income, access to capital, and control over cash flow reduce that risk. They don't eliminate uncertainty, but they narrow its impact on you.

Independence also changes how you think. When your income is tied to your own decisions, you become more disciplined and the Captain of your own destiny. Waste becomes clearly visible. Excuses disappear. Planning improves. You stop looking for guarantees and start building a solid foundation.

There is nothing glamorous about this process. It is incremental. It is repetitive. It requires consistency. But it works. Every strong business, every stable credit profile, every resilient entrepreneur arrives at the same place by taking the same kinds of steps, over time, without drama.

It's important to say this again clearly: independence does not require perfection. It requires commitment and taking action. You don't need to know everything. You don't need to be able to predict the future. You need to decide that you are going to roll up your sleeves and start today to become responsible for your own financial destiny. And then, start acting in alignment with that decision.

The tools you now understand, the right business structure, how the credit bureaus figure into the equation, the right corporate credit cards, lines of credit, and how to approach leasing and business credit risk management. These are practical business applications used every day by people who prefer knowledge and preparation over crossed fingers and hope.

Choosing independence is not loud. It does not announce itself. It shows up later, when the winds of financial adversity began blowing again. Other people will be out of a job and scrambling, and you are now the Captain of your own ship, and you're holding her steady as she goes when others are waiting in the unemployment line, or at the bank, with their hat in their hand, needing a loan. You are already positioned and funded. When others are surprised, you are ready.

This section exists to reinforce a simple truth: No one stumbles into independence. It is a chosen path.

Take Inventory: What Do You Know Now That You Didn't Know Before?

Before moving forward, it's worth stopping for a moment. Not to plan. Not to act. Just to take inventory.

Most books rush the ending. They pile on advice, urgency, or promises. That's not useful or necessary here. What matters now is the integration, what you've absorbed, what has shifted in your thinking, and what you can no longer unsee.

You didn't come this far to be entertained. You came to understand how money, credit, risk, and structure actually work. How to get your business the money it will need in the real world. Take a breath and ask yourself a few honest questions. What do you understand now about business credit that you didn't understand before?

Do you see more clearly how preparation changes outcomes?

How does access to capital before you need it alter decisions?

How does your business structure protect, or expose, you?

Think back to where you were when you opened this book. Were you confused? Cautious? Curious? Frustrated? Whatever brought you here is now part of the story. What matters is where you are now. There is a difference between information and insight. Information can be forgotten. Insight changes how you move. If something in these chapters made you uncomfortable, that's usually a sign it touched something real. Discomfort often appears right before growth.

This is also a good moment to assess your own habits honestly.

How do you currently handle money decisions? Do you delay them? Do you avoid them? Do you overthink them?

How do you respond to uncertainty? Do you freeze and do nothing? Do you charge into the unknown headfirst? Or do you prepare quietly?

There are no right answers here. There is only awareness.

Credit, business ownership, and independence are not moral achievements. They are practical ones. They reward planning and consistency, not intention. The systems described in this book do not care how motivated you feel. They respond to what you do consistently.

If you've now realized that parts of your financial life have been reactive rather than intentional, that's not failure. That's clarity, and that clarity is useful.

Much of what circulates around money and business is designed to provoke emotion, fear, excitement, outrage, and hope. Very little of it is designed to help you make better decisions.

What you've learned here is more subtle than that. Less dramatic and much more effective.

Strong credit profiles are built slowly. Stable businesses grow deliberately and steadily. Independence is assembled piece by piece.

Nothing about that process makes headlines. But it works.

If you're inclined, take a pen and write. Not necessarily your goals. Not affirmations. Just your observations.

What ideas in this book challenged assumptions you didn't realize you were carrying around with you?

What mistakes do you now perhaps recognize early enough to avoid?

What actions feel obvious now that once may have felt intimidating? Writing clarifies thinking. Thinking clarifies direction. There is no requirement to decide everything today. Reflection is not procrastination when it leads to alignment and action. The danger is reflection without movement. But movement without reflection and clarity is just, once again, noise.

This section exists to give you permission to pause without disengaging. To absorb without drifting. To prepare without rushing.

You don't need to be inspired. You need to be honest.

The Choice That Remains Is Now Yours

Every book ends. What matters is what happens after the last page.

There is no dramatic finish here because real life does not work that way. No music swells. No curtain drops. What happens next is quieter and far more important. You return to your life, your work, your responsibilities, and you decide what, if anything, changes.

This book was never meant to convince you of anything. It was meant to prepare you with knowledge. Preparation is subtle. It doesn't announce itself. It simply shows up later, when a decision needs to be made, and you are clearer, calmer, and better equipped than you were before.

You now understand how business credit actually works. You understand how risk is transferred, managed, or avoided. You understand why your business structure matters, why timing matters, and why waiting too long costs more than acting and perhaps making a mistake along the way.

From this point forward, inaction is no longer ignorance. It now becomes a choice. And choices have consequences, whether they are active or passive.

If you decide to move forward—starting a business, strengthening one, or building credit deliberately—you already know the steps. They are not mysterious. They require advance planning, patience, discipline, and consistency. None of that is glamorous. All of it is necessary and effective.

If you decide not to move forward right now, that is also a choice. Life allows it. Markets allow it. But understand it clearly for what it is: postponement and procrastination. An actual decision that you are making not to prepare to move your business forward financially at this time.

The purpose of preparation is not urgency. It is readiness.

There will be moments ahead, opportunities, disruptions, conversations, where what you learned here quietly matters: when a lender asks the right question, when a good business deal appears unexpectedly, when conditions tighten, and others are surprised … You are prepared. Those moments are where preparation pays its quiet dividends.

This book does not promise absolute certainty about anything. Nothing honest written by man ever does. What it offers is something better: personal agency. The ability to respond instead of react. The ability to decide intelligently instead of hoping you get it right.

If you choose to seek guidance, seek it deliberately. Ask better questions. Expect accountability. Pay attention to incentives. Whether that guidance comes from a consultant, a banker, a lawyer, or your own experience, remember that responsibility cannot be outsourced, only informed and learned.

And if you choose to move forward alone, that is also valid. Many of the strongest businesses are built quietly, without fanfare, by people who simply do the work persistently and refuse to quit.

Before you close this book, take one last moment.

Not to plan 10 steps ahead. Not to predict the future.

Just to answer one question, honestly, for yourself:

What is the next best thing I can do, starting today, to take control of my financial future and my own destiny with what I now know?

Write it down if you need to. Sit with it. You don't owe anyone a fast decision. You owe yourself clarity of action to make a decision to become the very best at whatever you decide to do.

Whatever you choose, choose consciously.

That awareness, more than any tactic, system, or strategy, is what separates people who continually repeat less than successful cycles from those who move forward and actually succeed.

This concludes the book. If you made it this far, and you have a question(s), I can answer, send me an email message to: jg@wilshirefinancialgroup.com. Put on top in the subject line of the message: *Hey JG, I finished reading the book!* Then, in the body of the message, list your questions, and I'll personally read them and send you my written responses free of charge.

Would you like to speak with me one-on-one, in depth, on any business topic or engage my copywriting services to advance your business? Please feel free to contact Eagle House Publications at **1+(888) 383-5318**, and my virtual assistant will schedule a consultation with me at my hourly rate of $750 (one hour minimum) and make the payment arrangements.

Please provide in advance the business topic you wish to discuss, and give me your three (3) best days and the best time of day in your schedule that will work for you. I will confirm the specific day and time of our conference call via email.

Afterward, on that day, I will call you in person, and we can speak about any business topic you wish or discuss any specific business-related questions you may have.

Yours for success,

John Garry